RE-
BONDING

RE-BONDING

Preventing and Restoring Damaged Relationships

Donald M. Joy, Ph.D.

WORD PUBLISHING
Dallas · London · Sydney · Singapore

Library of Congress Cataloging in Publication Data

Joy, Donald M. (Donald Marvin), 1928-
    Re-bonding: preventing and restoring damaged relationships.

    Bibliography:p.
    1. Christian life—Methodist authors. 2. Interpersonal relations—Religious aspects—Christianity. 3. Sex—Religious aspects—Christianity. 4. Reconciliation—Religious aspects—Christianity. 5. Intimacy (Psychology) I. Title.
BV4501.2.J685 1986   248.8′6   85—26012
ISBN 0-8499-3158-4

98FG987654321

Printed in the United States of America

For
David and Vicki
our beloved adoptees, stars of Chapter One
who have taught us as much as we have taught them
about grace, fidelity, and family

And to the host of people who have
shared our home and our hearts:

The occasional and temporary "live-in" sons and daughters;
Our international children,
Arturo and Adelina Parra of San Andres Island, Colombia
Soyon Lee of Seoul, Korea
Jonathan Muzamani Chauke of Harare, Zimbabwe

The Winona Lake FMY crowd from 1958 to 1973

The congregations of
Cave Community Free Methodist Church
Rockwall Free Methodist Church

The host of convention, retreat, and workshop participants

The "brown bag" lunch groups
which became "spiritual formation" contract groups ten
years ago and, finally,

The more than 2,000 students whose paths have
intentionally crossed mine in classes at
Asbury Theological Seminary

and also during guest professor tours at

Princeton Theological Seminary
Rosemead and Talbot Graduate Schools at Biola
Trinity Evangelical Divinity School
Wheaton Graduate School
since I was ushered into my "fourth estate" of teaching.

Contents

△

Foreword

△

WARNING: *This Book May Be Dangerous to Your Stereotypes!*

Not only that, it may also be dangerous to your daily schedule for a day or two—or longer. Professor Joy has created a book which "pulls you along." It is difficult to put down, not only because it is so engaging and stimulating to both thought and feeling, to memory and imagination, but because you begin to wonder where you are going to run into yourself again!

Re-bonding is one of those rare books in which every person will discover something of the unique dynamics of his or her own life. It may not always be a comfortable discovery. In fact, it may be a painful and disturbing revelation—a sensitive and insightful disclosure of deeply hidden dynamics of brokenness. At such points, however, the book opens doors into the recovery of wholeness.

Back to your stereotypes. This book focuses primarily on the wholeness of human life and relationships at the deepest level of being human—our sexuality. This in itself may disturb many of your stereotypes. But as Dr. Joy reminds us, the first thing the Bible says about the human creation is that God made them "male and female." This means that our sexuality is intimately, perhaps even intrinsically, involved in our being made in the image of God. If so, our sexuality is vitally involved in our fulfillment of the responsibilities of being created to transmit and project that image.

Re-bonding will confront your stereotypes about love, courtship, marriage, male-female and husband-wife relationships. It will challenge you to a sensitivity to the sexual dimensions of your relationship with God, and open your awareness of how intimate spiritual experiences heighten all the affective dimensions of our being—especially the sexual. For instance, discover why some leading Christian counselors often urge courting couples *not* to pray together!

Another group of stereotypes in danger of being shattered involves our perceptions of sexual deviancy. A whole new angle of vision is available here—one which emerges from a very holistic view of life. This includes excellent treatments of adultery, fornication, and divorce.

Stereotypes on dating and courtship will be deeply disturbed by this book. A whole new dimension of the dynamics of dating will be terribly damaging to long-held shibboleths. For example, learn why "date around" may be the most dangerous and destructive advice you could give your teen-age children.

Perhaps the most threatened group of stereotypes will be those held by many Christians. Dr. Joy provides startling new depths of insight on Scripture passages dealing with sexuality that go far beyond the narrow confines within which they are usually interpreted. He also brings into the discussion passages not usually associated with sexuality. Through this larger, more holistic exposition, he greatly expands our awareness of the total biblical picture of human sexuality.

Other stereotypes which are endangered and may be transformed by *Re-bonding* include those concerned with nudity, pornography, and virginity. For example, how can a promiscuous person become a virgin? What is the biblical precedent for such an offer?

Dr. Joy has written a book that speaks forcefully to the perverted and destructive sexuality of our age. He offers you tools with which to make your own diagnosis of the problem. But he also sets the problem itself within a perspective that points the way out of our bondage to brokenness and into the wholeness for which we were created and to which we can return in Jesus.

Re-bonding may disturb, disrupt, damage, and destroy any comfortable stereotypes behind which you hide the brokenness of your own sexuality. It will probe, penetrate, point out, and proscribe the root causes of your brokenness. And it will provide prescriptions for healing and paths into wholeness—from wherever you are.

Here is a book for every prisoner of our cultural captivity to broken sexuality. Every pastor, counselor, youth worker, teacher, parent, and young person should read this book.

Re-bonding may be dangerous to your stereotypes, but it could save your relationships, your courtship, your engagement, your marriage, and your family.

M. ROBERT MULHOLLAND, JR.
Dean, School of Theology
Associate Professor of New Testament
Asbury Theological Seminary

Acknowledgments

△

"Be Theirs My Special Thanks . . ."

Re-bonding . . . is a book I never intended to write. But when Floyd Thatcher and Ernie Owen followed me into the lobby of the Waco Hilton, the "conception" occurred. "You have another bonding book in you," one of them whispered. "We talked it over just now as you were presenting the key ideas of *Bonding: Relationships in the Image of God* to our sales reps."

"What are you talking about?"

"What you said about our misunderstandings about fornication, adultery, and Jesus' words about divorce. There are millions of hurting people out there who wonder if their lives can ever be put together again. We think you need another book that will deal with the tragedies people experience in their sexual experience."

At least those are the memories which rolled through my mind for the next few hours, and within a week, I mailed a prospectus to Ernie. I am so glad that these two sensitive executives saw right through my heart to a lot of people who are wanting to "put their lives together again."

But what I said on that winter day in Waco could never

have been formed in my understanding except for several major contributors who stand in my memory like "base coaches" who wave me on as I pass significant landmarks in my thought.

Pastor Mark Abbott, with whom I first worked when he was at Hamburg Wesleyan Church in New York, was the first pastor to empower me to open life's most intimate subjects to the ears of his people.

"I've booked you for a men's breakfast in the morning," he said as he picked me up at the Buffalo airport. "I want you to give them the male version of *The Total Woman*. I've called it *The Complete Man*."

"Well, I'd be glad to try something like that," I said, "but I haven't read Marabel Morgan yet."

"I thought of that possibility. Here's a copy. You can read it tonight in the Holiday Inn and go for it in the morning."

The next morning, I began my first talk by telling of the suddenness of the assignment. Then I said, "I've told your pastor, after reading *The Total Woman* last night, that I am not only ready to talk to you, I want to talk to your women, too." And I launched on a very different trajectory of defining both male and female identities, but of undergirding their relationships in the doctrines of Creation and Redemption in a way I might never have done before.

That was about a dozen years ago or more. I have worked with Pastor Abbott at Houghton College Wesleyan Church, and more recently at Seattle Pacific University's First Free Methodist Church where he is pastor. But the poetic brush strokes in our common vision reached a climactic point when Mark Abbott, novice to the denomination, drew the assignment to chair the revision subcommittee which processed the several versions of my General Conference resolutions targeted to change "the church's position on divorce." If his Friday night impromptu assignment seemed to me a bit presumptuous, imagine the load that fell on him to facilitate debate and refinement and final acceptance of a major change in the Free Methodist *Book of Discipline* as it defines "the church's position on divorce."

And here the plot is further grounded. I could never have evoked the attention of Ernie Owen and Floyd

Thatcher in Waco if I had not saturated myself in what the Bible teaches about divorce. And I had done that under the enormous weight of grief that my denomination, which claims everywhere to ground its doctrine in Scripture and especially to be sensitive to the teachings of Jesus, was, in fact, clearly in violation of the teaching and behavior of Jesus regarding divorced people and about the so-called "grounds for divorce." You can unpack the details of my conclusions in chapter four, "Grounds for Divorce?"

And it was Professor Joseph Wang, along with Pastor Arthur Brown and Professor James Mannoia, who met regularly in my office for Friday fast lunches late in 1983 and into 1984 to discuss denominational concerns, especially invoking grace on the General Conference of 1985. It was in one of those sessions that Dr. Brown agonized that the church's position on divorce was most difficult to administer. We discovered that anyone trapped in divorce would, technically, be better off to forfeit membership and to reapply as a "sinner" than to try to deal with the tragedy within the community of faith. But it was Dr. Wang who literally leaped to the front of his chair at Dr. Brown's opening statement, and exclaimed, "That's right. The *Discipline* does not even know the plain teaching about fornication and adultery. So the church is teaching wrong things about divorce!" His delightful Chinese-English amazed us, evoking a powerful summons to action.

I began, then, to develop the resolution that went through many scholarly hands for review, and eventually circulated to delegates known to me. Superintendent Theodore Johnson of North Michigan and Superintendent Darrold Hill of Wabash Conference responded by "authoring" modified resolutions which incorporated major swatches of the one developed here. It was the North Michigan bill, amended and refined by two levels of revision committees, that was adopted.

But there is a missing chapter. During my doctoral program at Indiana University, I intentionally enrolled in a course in "adolescent development" taught by Boyd McCandless. It was a summer intensive, complicated by Professor McCandless's contracting serum hepatitis from an accidental injury involving a zip knife he was using to strip up a revised edition of one of his books. But it was his straightforward description of adolescent sexuality that caught my full attention. I recall his saying that while the adolescent is fully equipped for sexual experience, it is inevitable that any sexual encounter before marriage will leave irreparable scars. All of that was impressive, and his data were grounded in empirical research, but I became, almost unwittingly, a part of his data. He required a "sexual history" of all of us, which, he said, he needed to pore over for use as a partial base for a forthcoming book. The request to "construct your entire sexual history" was at once frightening and likely impossible. But I tried. It ran to perhaps forty pages. I made a carbon copy. Dr. McCandless went over it with me, showing a complete and sensitive reading of the entire document. But it was traumatic for me. I burned my copy in the Campus View apartment incinerator.

But I was also liberated by having put together my entire remembered sexual history. And I do not hesitate to encourage anyone now to reconstruct theirs. I often help with a timeline and secret symbols for typical misadventures. Who was it who said, "The unexamined life is not worth living"? And it is certainly true that God's grace cannot go where we close the doors and refuse to "come home to the truth" through repentance—which is a bit like doing a "history."

In my present world, Dr. Robert Mulholland, my colleague and friend, and now my Dean, is a critical specialist both in the biblical text and in its interpretation. He gave me most helpful feedback on the General Conference resolution. But his campus sensation here is *"NT 666: The Book of Revelation."* Unlike many "left-brained" approaches to the book which tend to crash and burn on technicalities, Bob's teaching focuses on the images and their interpretation, inductively, from the text itself. In my fifteen years here I have audited two other of my colleagues' courses, but this one is next on my list. Bob was good enough to check a major exposition I constructed from the images of the Great Harlot and of the Bride dressed in white. The extensive essay I developed on these images was a significant piece of homework necessary for the flow and message of this book. Dean Mulholland made significant suggestions which cleared my thoughts both on promiscuity and on purity. And it must be every professor's dream that his Dean would consent to write a guest foreword. How gracious!

I salute Dr. Mulholland also and congratulate him on his election to the position of Dean of the Faculty of the Theological School at Asbury Theological Seminary. The election tells everyone something of the quality of scholarship and the quality of teaching that is the guiding vision at Asbury. But it also carries with it a notice to the world about the nature of this unique environment. Here, as in no other environment in which I have worked, rigorous scholarship is combined with vital commitment to community. Here professors are supported and enabled to teach, to write, and to advance their professional development in a way that is unique. But here, too, the entire campus is a community of prayer, of encouragement, and of simple Christian grace. The "spiritual formation" program, entirely voluntary, has led us to newer and deeper levels of community which knows no bounds of status or age or position. In my career here, it has been easy to salute President David L. McKenna and President Emeritus Frank Bateman Stanger. These great statesmen have created and sustained Asbury Theological Seminary as a uniquely effective free-standing community of knowledge and spiritual formation.

I owe special debts of a more specialized sort to several people.

Al Bryant, at Word, Inc., is easily the gentlest and quickest editor with whom I have ever worked.

Dr. James Dobson put me on his famous *Focus on the Family* radio show in the early eighties, and continues to honor me with guest appearances. Our enormous common ground, much of it unknown to even his wider public, has made our new acquaintance a great blessing to me.

My son, John M. Joy, psychiatric social worker and ordained minister, gave the manuscript a most rigorous reading. From his work in rehabilitative therapy, he gave special sensitivity to the "sexual addiction" perspective. And it is to John I owe the contact with Sexual Addicts Anonymous, and the questionnaire in the Appendix.

Dorian Luckenbill Joy, our daughter by marriage, must have given me the most deeply affective reading of all. Her excellent and extensive notes on the manuscript are continuing evidence of the mutual trust we have shared with Dorian. Her reading of *Re-bonding* was enhanced by her empathic concern for people in trouble, and she read it, no doubt with tears, wanting her friends and acquaintances who need the book so much not to be unnecessarily offended by my language or argumentation.

Vicki and David, recipients of the dedication, also read and noted problems and typos in the text. Their separate and poetically reunited pilgrimages give them unusual grounding of authority for affirming the dictum: "God who has created all things good can make all things new, through Jesus."

Robbie reads my stuff "hot off the Hewlett Packard"! That "virginal reading" can happen only once, so she corrects my language, images, and theological/technical sense in a first round that is always kind, usually straightforward, but inevitably motivating.

Last of all, I salute the Spring 1985 class, "CE 628: Discipleship Development in the Home." They were the first to read *Bonding: Relationships in the Image of God*, instead of hearing me work with those ideas orally. But they also were the first to hear and see much of *Re-bonding: Preventing and Restoring Damaged Relationships*. I have even cited some of them in the footnotes. That class was surely a microcosm of this "community of faith and scholarship." Perhaps I should apologize to the forthcoming Spring 1986 class. They will be confronted now with two bonding books, and must be the first to hear much of what Robbie and I are now putting together in *Lovers: Whatever Happened to Eden?*

Introduction

△

"Where Were You When I Was Fifteen?"

I grew up with a deeply ingrained "moral sense." For a long time I assumed it was my parental and church environment which was totally responsible for that moral sense. But by delaying two of my advanced graduate programs until midlife, I had the good fortune to come to my reading and my research with a better set of questions than I might have mustered in my twenties. All of this led me to believe this: God has so endowed humans that a sense of "righteousness" expressed as a sense of fairness and justice is universal among naive humans. And I must admit that some of the "moral teaching" I absorbed in my environment collided very early with that intrinsic sense of "what is truly fair and right"—a naive expression of "righteousness."

Let me illustrate. Perhaps your experience matches mine.

Forty-two years ago Russ was "sleeping around." At least that is what he told me week after week in "Intro to Sociology" class and at piano ensemble practice. He named the girls, quoted their "come ons," and offered me advice if I wanted to make it with the preacher's daughter I was dating. I married at nineteen, he at twenty-two. And when his wedding came off it was quite a celebration. There may have been a few whispered suspicions that his wife might not know all about his pre-marital misadventures, but all in all, he made it into marriage with a clean reputation in the community.

It was different for Bob. He and Verna were married almost without announcement in late May at the end of their second year of college. The community pipeline predicted a six-month pregnancy, and by Christmas they were parents. I learned not long ago from Bob that he burst in on one of our professors early that spring and blurted out the embarrassing, shame-filled story of the pregnancy. The sensitive, devout Christian teacher said to him, in terms I instinctually know now were right: "Are you wanting to end the relationship with Verna?" "Not at all," Bob had sobbed, "I want to marry her in the worst way, but we promised this would never happen, and it did. I feel so ashamed." Forty years later Bob told me how the prof then said, "Well, we have some problems, but we do not have a major tragedy. You and Verna want to establish your own home. We could wish that everything had happened on the schedule that matched your dreams. But will you bring Verna in? I think we have some news to break to both sets of parents. I will help you with that." And he did, marshalling the full support of both families behind Bob and Verna.

Even today, however, in the scattered campus community of more than four decades ago, a cloud hangs over their marriage and some classmates would be ready to confirm that little Mary, who is now past forty, was "conceived out of wedlock."

Russ is largely out of mind. He was clever enough to "cover his tracks" or blackmail the women he used, sealing their lips. So his reputation is less tarnished in memory than Bob's.

I was baffled then at the unfairness of it all. Russ was a rascal who "kept his nose clean." Bob and Verna "got caught." Yet it was evident from every measure that Bob and Verna had won the integrity competition hands down. I took "Intro to Sociology" and lived on the same dormitory

floor with both Russ and Bob. The three of us did basketball
lay-ups, free throws, and scrimmages together. Yet never
once did Bob suggest that he was consumed by sexual desire.
He sometimes listened to Russ as he bragged about a recent
conquest. I wonder now whether Bob's imagination was
fueled by Russ's vivid reporting. It didn't help the innocent
vision, I'm certain.

Perhaps most telling of all, Russ, a child of divorce, is
now in his fourth marriage. Bob and Verna maintain a family
center that has already launched two healthy adult children,
with two more on the college years runway.

I wept in my heart for both Bob and Russ. They were
my friends. But I was stung then by the public humiliation
the most honorable man attracted to himself. Russ would
have, and perhaps did, walk away from sexual irresponsibility, covering his tracks. It was not as easy then as it is today
with a confidential abortion to pay for secretly, or worse,
to leave to the young woman to handle alone.

I found myself making a hypothetical choice as a young
father of two sons. Robbie and I were up to our ears in
ministry with teens during much of their childhood. So our
family prayers and our private anguish sometimes sur-
rounded teenagers in trouble. My daydreaming choice was
between two horrors: "If I had to choose whether one of
my sons would be a playboy or would fail to make it to
the church on time, which would it be?" The answer, violat-
ing popular values (and my covert moral teaching for forty
years), came out clearly, "I would rather have to deal with
a monogamous impulse that jumped the gun."

But it was purely moral instinct that prompted me to
opt for the second of the problems. Now, more recently,
I have begun to see that I had almost completely misunder-
stood the clear biblical teachings about such things as fornication and adultery. And with my flawed understanding,
I was using the terms improperly until well past the age
of fifty!

Caught in the trap in which popular morality seemed
in conflict with the reality of personal integrity, it was the
painful ambiguity that I felt which stung me most. Since
age eighteen, as president of the student body at a small

college, I have found myself almost helplessly "a man for others." What a tragedy that when my friends unloaded their current tragedies on me I did not know what I know today. I apologize to them, many of whom still respect me as we treasure long-term friendships. On the other hand, I celebrate that the intrinsic "sense of justice" tended to dominate even when my popular misunderstanding of Scripture and the Christian faith was still naive and distorted.

As a pastor, then as a director, with Robbie, of a large church youth ministry, I have always been ready to hear and to respond to the unvarying sexual turbulences of the young.

More recently, helped by some bold alumni who asked me to their churches to speak openly to the real issues of family life, I have gone public with some of the responses I have given in private. On one occasion, following a men's breakfast in Toronto, where I had leveled with school-aged boys and their fathers and grandfathers, the first question in the discussion that followed came from a distinguished gray-haired man. He rose, cleared his throat, and said, "Dr. Joy, I have a question for you." My heart leaped. I thought, *Here it is! He's going to blow me out of the water for being so sexually explicit.* Then he went on, "Where were you when I was fifteen?"

"When you were fifteen we couldn't have talked about these things, in church or anywhere, likely. But a pornographic age has written the curriculum for us and has forced us out of our lethargy and driven us back to Scripture and into the arms of God crying for help. On the other hand," I continued, "when you were fifteen most of what I have told you this morning was not known by anybody anywhere." Then I told him of a small collection on my library shelf of some of the "sex education" books from the turn of the century. One cannot read them without chuckling, I said, because the best information then was, by present knowledge, absolutely false.

In a very different setting in East Texas, I sat in on a Saturday evening "talk back" session at a youth retreat weekend where I spoke to some 1,200 teens from the area. One of the counselors, with her husband, posed the toughest question I have ever faced:

"Dr. Joy. As I listen to your addresses, I try to imagine whether Jesus would use the words you use and talk about the things you talk about."

"Oh, I have offended you," I said. "I wouldn't try to justify what I do, but I need to apologize for offending you."

Just then a pair of high school women, on opposite sides of the large circle, leaped dangerously forward on their folding chairs, both interrupting the counselor. One of them blurted out:

"Don't stop him. All my life I have been attending church and this weekend is the first time anybody has helped me to see my own life in relation to what God expects of me."

I turned to the counselor. "How old were you when you were converted to Christ?" I asked.

"Five years ago, when I was twenty-eight."

"Do you have any idea what your teen-aged years might have been like if you had been living in obedience to Jesus then?"

"No."

"Then maybe we should go ahead and help the young Christians deal with the pressing issues they are living out." And we continued.

What the counselor and her husband likely could not have known, and perhaps would have signaled the young woman that she had better never share, was this. The young interrupter had an abortion when she was fifteen. She had told me privately that she now felt betrayed by her United Methodist Church for not helping her to find the words of Jesus and the teachings of the Bible that would have prepared her to take responsibility for her sexuality as a young Christian.

For twenty years or so now, I have been going public with evidences I have collected. But there is a growing crescendo of celebration as I bring together all that the Bible says with all that my most sensitive intrinsic sense of justice says about the real, concrete world. Sometimes

I feel so comfortable that I am tempted to cry out with Simeon, that aging man who lived to see Jesus: "Lord, now let your servant depart in peace!"

But until then, I will go on reporting on the best of my understanding to the widest possible audiences. *Re-bonding: Preventing and Restoring Damaged Relationships* is the second in a series of three books in which I am offering my best perceptions at this time. Check the copyright date; I will be "further up and further in" as C. S. Lewis would say, if you are reading this more than three or four years after that date.

Next year look for the third title which will round out the bonding series. Robbie and I are now preparing it. We are tentatively calling it *Lovers: Whatever Happened to Eden?*

DONALD M. JOY, PH.D.
*Professor of Human Development and
    Christian Education
Asbury Theological Seminary
Wilmore, Kentucky*

RE-
BONDING

1

The Mystery of Human Bonding

△

Toward the end of April, twenty-five-year-old David stayed behind after the spiritual formation group broke to leave my office. "I suddenly feel so naive," he confided, "like I was about fifteen! I've lived at home, my parents have paid my bills, I haven't needed to carry money, and even in the summers when I've had a job, I never cashed my checks, I turned them over to Mom. But I have such a feeling now that I need to be on my own. I just want to sit down with Dad and Mom tonight and tell them that next fall I'm going to move onto campus when I start my second master's degree. And I'm going to pay my own way somehow."

"They'll be glad to hear that," I said, no doubt reflecting my own parental delight when my sons had married at nineteen and twenty and had rather quickly taken off with a lot of maturity and good judgment in the use of the scarce financial resources we helped them scrape together so "two could live as cheaply as one."

"You don't know my dad," David cautioned me.

It took a midnight conference with his parents to announce and discuss his decision to take responsibility for his own life. Then, with that decision behind him, a surprise overtook him. He told the formation group, "At 7:05 in

3

the evening, while I was sitting in the library, I was suddenly taken aback. Three years before I had done a tragic thing. I had broken up with Victoria at the very point in our relationship that I should have asked her to marry me." This insight hit him just forty-eight hours after taking responsibility for his adult life.

But Vicki was now living in California. David could locate her address easily enough, but four single women sharing an apartment left no easily traceable telephone listing. It took two days to reach her and surprise her on the phone. David told her of the sudden memory of the tragic break-up. "I should have asked you to marry me, Vicki, and I'm calling you now to ask. Will you?"

Silence engulfed the telephone connection. Then out of the night came Vicki's response, "There is a God." Then finally, "Yes, David, I will marry you. I should tell you that I need time to pray about it, but I will marry you."

I met Victoria near the end of May. David hitched a ride with me as I drove to a retreat site only forty miles from her Midwestern hometown. She was to arrive within hours of our schedule, ending a cross continental drive with a roommate. Vicki arrived on Saturday morning and I walked into my suite to find these two beautiful people sitting on my couch. They looked like young lovers who had just become engaged after a two-year university romance. During the next four hours the three of us spent together, I moved to quench a deep curiosity. I asked the obvious question, looking at this peaceful, grace-filled young woman:

"How did you stay single, Vicki, living and working in the Lake Arrowhead community with its population of Campus Crusade men?"

"In a way, it wasn't easy," she replied. "I have refused two proposals within the last year, but I had promised myself that I would never marry any man unless I was as deeply attached to him as I had become to David. And I never felt that kind of love for anyone except David."

I've wondered what it was that was holding Vicki in the deep "subsoil" of David's memory since the break-up three years before. And how do you account for Vicki's developing a "standard" by which to measure all future relationships and by which she managed to refuse two proposals? It is easy enough to label it "true love," or even "romance," but the mystery is profoundly deeper than such simple labels suggest.

David had discussed a casual friendship during our early months of contact. I had questioned him about why he did not move to date a young woman with whom he often studied in the library. Their friendship was nicely playful, but he had never moved toward intentional dating, not even once. I now suspect that it was the bond with Vicki which, quite below his awareness, was holding him back. David had named Victoria in a single breath in the spiritual formation group when he told of his "first intimate friendship" in the "breaking away" agenda with which we spent several weeks introducing ourselves. Each of us, in that confidential setting committed to mutual support and mutual respect, opened our histories by recounting the basic shape of our lives in what Daniel Levinson has called "the age twenty transition."[1]

I want to use the term "bonding" to describe the mystery of human attachment between two persons. It is so profound a mystery that it cannot be understood merely in physiological terms. It includes biological, psychological, spiritual, even ethical dimensions. By pair bonding, I wish to refer to that exclusive, lifelong, mutually attaching relationship in which a woman and a man form one new entity, a sort of composite, corporate identity and personality. In such a case, while each retains individuality and integrity as a separate, distinct person, they together form a "persona" both greater than and different from the sum of the two parts. I went to great lengths to define various sorts of human bonding in *Bonding: Relationships in the Image of God.*

When I was thirteen, I was in love. And while it ended when I was fourteen, quite abruptly, I suspect that its positive effects are still with me and, no doubt, form an affectional structure which both contributes to my sense of "self," and my deep attachment to my wife, Robbie. I was not even to meet Robbie until I was seventeen, five years after I first "fell in love" with Ann.

My age thirteen romance was with a fourteen-year-old

woman. Since I was in Kansas, I was licensed to drive a car, so I picked her up on the half-dozen or so formal dates I could arrange before a senior man, Richard Anton, snatched her away. They were married after he graduated and she finished high school as a married woman. We continued to find ourselves playing opposites in the high school operettas and riding in the same van as we went to instrumental and vocal contests and to audition for scholarships at nearby colleges. When Richard stole my first love away, I grieved. My parents scolded me but never mocked me. I lost ten pounds in a month. But when Richard and Ann married, I began to reconstruct my life. That was more than forty years ago, and the Anton children, since the tragic loss of both parents, have graciously extended their respect in a special way to Robbie and me. Their youngest, John, came to live with us and attend college not long after the family had called on me to preside at the double funeral of Richard and Ann.

I tell the story of childhood romance because any significant relationship which moves on *eros* sets up the beginning "sticky surface" which might eventually yield a lifelong, exclusive attachment and the formation of a new united personality. My parents were supportive of all of my friendships, and "having a girlfriend" seemed to be well within the range of good behavior at my home.

These early and innocent loves are instinctually distant. The child who has not been seduced or exploited by someone else brings a naive simplicity to the early relationships and my loss of ten pounds from the sheer nausea of losing someone beautiful and important to me seems incredible now. Ann and I never touched or kissed. It was enough that we knew we "owned" each other in that special "boy-friend-girlfriend" way that children have. And it was almost too much that we sometimes sat at extreme opposite ends of the bench seat of my dad's 1935 Plymouth. As we each crowded against the doors on opposite sides, we were excited, almost speechless, with the intimacy that we had won.

"Puppy love" and "infatuation" are labels which tend to be used by older folks to put down the young. So in this discussion I wish to regard all feelings of human attachment as being out of the same root. I will be working on the assumption that whether the persons are old or young is irrelevant and that the use of these demeaning labels tells us more about the people who use them than about the people they think they are describing.

I stand in awe, even reverence, of the gift of bonding. And I regard all forms of human attachment as operating on the capital of that enormous gift: the ability to inhabit the world of another person and to be caught up in the joint adventures of life. When this attachment is mutual, the two of them are virtually immune to our efforts to distract them, to break them up, or to humiliate them with our immature and demeaning labels. And even if we separate them by space and time, the bond that has begun to form may very well be indestructible.

Metaphysical Grafting: Eros

This phenomenon of "bonding" which exists between lovers refers simply to the attraction that eventually and almost physically and literally attaches two persons "as one." When we see them clinging to each other, it is their signal to us that they want this relationship to become permanent, exclusive, and lifelong.

I am calling the bonding "metaphysical" because it cannot be explained simply in biological categories. Bonding is clearly a matter both of the body and of the "heart," that affective center which, however real it may be, is beyond being measured in physical terms.

Bonding is a "grafting" because "two become one," not only in a physical sense, but in a deeper melting together of minds and personalities. Bonding brings a fusing of two persons, their vocations, their dreams, their futures, their property, everything. And the metaphysical grafting—this melding of two into one—occurs without a contract, without deliberate choice, simply by the otherwise ordinary exchanges that might have occurred between an infinite number of pairings of possible friends.

When we see this *eros*-based grafting taking place, we often describe it as being "blind." We say, "What does she see in him?" It is of little comfort to prospective in-laws that this unlikely man will one day become the father of their adorable and gifted grandchildren!

And the parents are right. She is blind to the truth about him as he now exists. Affectional bonding looks through the tinted lenses of perfection and possibilities. Love sees through the beloved. How else could two acne-covered teens persist in their building of a powerful bond? Or, for that matter, how could two octogenarians bear the physical realities of their arthritic bodies unless they were captivated by a love that sees through and into the special qualities of the beloved person?

"Take a good look at the next Greyhound load of senior citizens you see at the rest stop," I caution my college friends. "Ask yourself which of those bodies is most like the one you will inhabit when you are seventy-five. And will you be loved unconditionally by someone then?" I ask them, and the auditorium becomes quiet. "Be sure that you really come to 'know' your beloved and that the bond is well tended. And if it is, then you will only ripen with age, and your mellowness will hold the powerful magnet of affection firmly in place 'till death do you part.' "

While *eros* alone is an insufficient basis for lifelong faithfulness, it provides the mysterious original "glue" which enhances and empowers a truly great love. For most of my life I had equated *eros* with mere sexual passion. Imagine my surprise in finding that it is among the most holy of all emotions—that of "desire" and "devotion." And since the most painful of human failures comes in the affectional arena, sexual tragedies and comedies have diverted our attention from the deeper meaning of *eros*.

I wish I could say that it was my studies of New Testament Greek which opened my eyes on *eros*—which made me look again at *philia* and at *agape*, as well. My awakening came at the Lexington Sheraton Inn on Friday, 8 October 1976. I had responded to an invitation from the Kentucky Humanities Council about which I knew nothing but with which I would later serve as a director for four years. The invitation heralded the famous Professor William

Arrowsmith from Yale, who would be lecturing on images from English literature which serve the humanities and all of us. I filed an absence plan with my Dean and took off from teaching for a half-day. Arrowsmith spoke twice, with lunch in between. I was annoyed at the shabby behavior of some young university professors who harassed him at each discussion period. But the indelible moment for me came when he cited lines from Sophocles's classic *Philoctetes*. Sophocles built his plot around the famous magic bow and arrows which the gods used to ignite the fire on Mount Oeta. The sacred bow and arrows are kept, according to the legend, in a secret vault to prevent their falling into the hands of enemies of Troy, for the ancient city's invulnerability is locked into the bow and arrows. The young Neoptolemus approaches Philoctetes.

"Is this, in your hands, the famous bow?"

"Yes, this, this in my hands."

"May I see it closer? Touch and adore it like a god?"

Philoctetes responds, "You may have it and anything else of mine that is for your good."

To which Neoptolemus confesses, "I long for it, yet only with such longing that if it is lawful, I might have it, else let it be."[2]

Suddenly there it was. *Eros* is adoration, and at its highest levels it is fully sanctified of self-interest and exploitation. My old "hierarchy" of loves was exploded, for *eros* was suddenly capable of the highest moral purity. I was not then prepared for the clear New Testament proof that *agape* is also susceptible to the grossest selfishness, but more of that later.

Sometimes some unhappy wizard will try to pass off on us the idea that true love "consumes itself" in the process of loving, and eventually survives with little feeling at all. In that picture of "true love," the mature lover is an impartial witness to a great love which has now faded, leaving only withered seeds.

I suspect that Ortega y Gasset is nearer to the truth when he observes that "a love which has sprung from the roots of a person in all likelihood cannot die. It is forever grafted to the sensitive soul."[3]

Gasset goes on to assert that circumstances such as distance or time may prevent two lovers tending and nourishing their love, in which case, he says, it may lose its force. Even so, it is only transformed into "a sentimental wisp," a fond memory, "a slight vein of emotion which will continue to pulsate in the subsoil of consciousness." But, he says, "it will not die: its sentimental quality will remain intact."

If Gasset is right, then the "grafting" of bonded love is indestructible. "Life on this planet will never be the same again," a young man once confided when he realized that his beloved was abandoning him. Ask a surviving spouse after the death of a mate: the bond survives even death. So when lovers are separated—for whatever reasons—something of the relationship survives "in the subsoil of consciousness" and all of life will be colored by that memory, that emotion, that "sentimental wisp." And when the separation is an unavoidable riptide which tears at the emotions of the two of them, they remain together, in spite of time and space. Gasset describes this transcendent character of metaphysical bonding: "It means being with the other vitally. The most exact, but too technical phrase would be this: an ontological state of being with the beloved, faithful to its destiny, no matter what it is." In this view, he says, a woman who loves a thief, regardless of where her body may be, is with her senses in his jail.

Elsewhere, I have traced the twelve steps that go into a typical "pair bond."[4] Here, it is enough to trace the pattern so familiar to humans everywhere:

Eye to body. Amazing! Where have you been all my life? What a spectacular creation! Why is my heart pounding?

Eye to eye. Involuntarily, I cannot keep my eyes off of you, and I do not even yet know your name.

Voice to voice. What was that again? I missed your name. You're joking? You couldn't be. I'm absolutely serious. Would I tease you?

Hand to hand. Hang on! We're packing through this crowd as "one"! It is important that we stick together.

Arm to shoulder. It's us against the world. Or, maybe,

for "our side." Two count more than each alone. It is definitely us!

Arm to waist. Move closer. We've got a lot to talk about. Tell me your best visions about the future. Tell me we are together in your longest dreams.

Face to face. "Drink to me only with thine eyes." Don't say anything, I can read everything and you know what I'm thinking, too.

Hand to head. I've never felt so safe. With other people I'm nervous if they sit behind me, looking over my shoulder, but you may have my face, my ears, my hair, the nape of my neck. I'm comfortable with you.

Hand to body. I will take care of you, and I accept you with the peculiar shape of your whole body. Your imperfections have become your trademarks to me. I would know those hands and the back of your neck with its hair follicle pattern anywhere.

Mouth to breast. I salute you. You who will be the mother of our children. I myself draw my strength from you; you have formed my sense of identity, and I am not embarrassed to place myself in a dependent relationship to you.

Hand to genital. Everything is yours. I've known all along that we were made for each other.

Genital to genital. One at last. How could I have known that I was created for this moment and for all of the moments it guarantees to us?

It would be easy to stop here and to say that this "grafting" by *eros* is all there is. And it is almost enough. The magic of "seeing through" a person to the possibilities is a supernatural vision, for it is God who sees us not as we are but as we might become. So lovers are given this Godlike power to call us to heights of being we otherwise would never have achieved. And it is C. S. Lewis who, making this point about love, observes that each of us bears the image of God in some profound way. That "image" is evident in that "the dullest and most uninteresting person you can talk to may one day be a creature which, if you saw it now, you would be strongly tempted to worship, or else a horror and a corruption such as you now meet, if at all, only in a nightmare."[5]

So let *eros* stand as the mysterious magnetic impulse to adore and to worship. Classical Greek uses *eros* in that way—to denote the awe and wonder one feels in the presence of sacred objects such as the sacred bow and arrows from Mount Oeta. As such, we become better aware of how the impulse to worship and the impulse to sexual love may be "wired on the same circuit."

Seeing Life Steadily and Whole: Philia

Eros either is grounded in friendship or must lead quickly to friendship love, or what the Greeks called *philia*. This second layer of love consists of "common interests." Most lovers meet because of common pursuits: the same school, the same workplace, the same event—these bring people together. So there is a screening that takes place ahead of the quickening of the heartbeat with *eros*. Mick came to faith at thirty-five, after an abused childhood in an alcohol-drenched home, after three marriages and sleeping with another six dozen women. Robbie and I took him along to Cincinnati to a weekend of church seminars I was conducting. He was amazed:

"I can't believe these kinds of people are in the world. Where have I been all of my life? Everybody wanted to know who I am, where I have been, what I am about. I've been looking in the wrong places. The only women I have found were ones I met in singles' bars, and they were all losers—just like me."

Maybe Mick was right: sometimes there is simply nothing to build on in a relationship, because there is no "common ground" except the anonymity of a singles' bar and the anesthesia of drugs and alcohol which prevents discovering the real person and the genuine spheres of interests. When this happens, people often make only the gestures of love, and tend to "pass like ships in the night." No one will ever know, perhaps, what rich potential was at their fingertips, since they opted for games instead of honest meeting.

Common ground, however, positions potential lovers "side by side," such that they do not become preoccupied with the other as an object. Cathy and Roger met while they were loaded down with heavy responsibility as counselors in separate trial families with me on the Sheltowee Trace during a hundred-mile backpacking trip. Each had responsibility for a half-dozen teens, including some inner city kids we had recruited for "discipleship development through trail camping," a course I teach through which to train people for ministry. Cathy was heavily involved in a house church in Lexington, well known for its radical evangelism and its social services: "Christ's Community . . ." it was called. She was fully committed to ministry and was finishing at the University of Kentucky enroute to seminary. Roger was shouldering the responsibility for Youth for Christ's inner city program in Cincinnati. You can see that their *philia* base was well established. One hundred miles of hiking in their separate groups, then an evening of vespers, dinner, and fatigue made tolerable by good conversation, set the stage for *philia* to expand and for *eros* to awaken. No one was surprised when the wedding invitations brought us together two years later for the high nuptial celebration.

Sometimes *philia* shows itself in the post-*eros* and pre-nuptial phase. Nowhere is such a sequence told more powerfully than by Sheldon Vanauken in *A Severe Mercy*. Here is a love story in which the author, "Van," and Jean, whom he calls "Davy," fall captive to *eros*, then turn quickly to completely reconstruct their lives to include the other. For example, they vow to read every book the other has read, so they will have a common base of experience. They erect a "shining barrier" to keep the whole outer world at bay while they construct their new persona within the citadel of love. Eventually the barrier closed them in to a sort of marital narcissism, nicely confronted by C. S. Lewis, their mentor and eventually their evangelist who brought them to Christian faith.[6]

The friendship dimension of love is a lifelong adventure. While each partner needs space "to be" and even to have a distinct life and vocation, the growing romance requires a sincere and consistent support of each other's interests. It is almost a measure of the mutuality of a marriage to examine it to see whether (a) each listens as much as they talk at the end of a day's work apart; and (b) each has a balanced set of spheres in which to work as the primary partner, tested by how each of them is introduced to new publics. For example, I am pleased to move with Robbie in circles in which my best credential is, "This is Robbie's husband; he teaches at Asbury Seminary."

In Sickness and in Health: Storge

What happens when illness and aging take their toll? *Eros*, of course, has a grounding in the deep subsoil. But it may be so preoccupied with the fantastic hopes for the future that it is indifferent to the present pain. So, in the traditional marriage ceremony, the officiant stabs the covenant to a deeper level: "Will you be faithful in sickness and in health?" And here we may be tapping a love that every parent knows: the absolute fidelity which expresses itself in nurturing and comforting ways. Parental love is *storge* in the spectrum of Greek love words.

Storge love says, "I will take care of you. Don't be afraid. Nothing bad can happen to you." It is the love which sees a parent through a hundred nights at the bedside of a child who is seriously ill or dying. All the while, the glue holds. You will see the stroking of the hands, the patting of the face, the light kissing on the cheek, the fondling of the hair. These would appear to be grounded in *eros*, but there is something here that is able to do "unilateral loving." The "one-way" gift of attention is spontaneous and unconditional, simply because the relationship exists. There must be the fleeting thought, though it is not a driving force in *storge*, "if the roles were to be exchanged, my partner would care for me in the same way." The phantom of reciprocity is not what energizes *storge*, but it is exacted of each in the traditional marriage litany.

In the Vanauken love story, Sheldon describes how he stood at her bedside in the final moments of her life: "I am here, Davy; I am with you," he whispered.

But there was no response.

Then she stirred. There was no change at all in her half-parted lips or eyes or the hand I held. But then her other hand and arm came slowly up from her side. I could not think what she was doing. The hand moved slowly across her. It found my face. She touched my brow and hair, then each eye in turn. Then my mouth. Her fingers moved to each corner of my mouth, as we had always done. And I gave her fingers little corner-of-the-mouth kisses, as we had always done. Then her arm fell slowly back. Past seeing and past speaking, with the last of her failing strength, she had said goodbye.[7]

Till Death Do Us Part: Agape

In the circle of our relatives and friends we are watching the tragic fading of life from both men and women who are victims of Alzheimer's disease. When a grinding destruction of disease and disability reduces a partner to the silent one who waits alone, then love comes to its "bottom line." Here is a deeper commitment than *eros* with its physiological "prompts" and vision of perfection. And here is a love which holds when the shared interests and mutualities of *philia* have evaporated. Even parental *storge* commitment to care and protection may finally crumble. But *agape* love is what Mildred Wynkoop likes to call "targeted affection." *Agape* chooses. And when it has chosen deliberately, it overrides feelings, even instincts.

Agape as "targeted affection" is not at all what many Christians have thought. It has no feeling, no sentiment, and represents the cool, detached determination to "go with a decision." It may even be a decision to move toward destructive ends: "Demas has forsaken me," St. Paul wrote, "having loved this present world," and the love word is this targeted *agape*. You can read this overlooked use of *agape* in Colossians 4:14. In this way, agape is the "bottom line," the binding contract.

In the famous exchange between Jesus and Peter following the resurrection, Jesus asks Peter whether Peter "loves" him, using *agape*. Peter is offended at this because Jesus asks twice using that "bottom line," "love as a choice" question, so Peter responds using the *philia* love: you know that I love you with shared vision and common interests. Eventually, it is Jesus who moves to the more feeling, affection-activated word and in the final question the two find each other's trust again, but it is at the *philia* level, which assumes the *agape* base, not the other way around. Look, here, at the exchange as recorded in John 21:15–17. If you are impatient with my rather nontraditional explanation, I am sympathetic. The traditional explanations have seemed quite unhelpful to many of us, too. I have transliterated the *agape* and *philia* words so you can trace the development for yourself:

> When they had finished eating, Jesus said to Simon Peter, "Simon, son of John, do you truly *agapas* me more than these?"
> "Yes, Lord," he said, "you know that I *philo* you."
> Jesus said, "Feed my lambs."
> Again Jesus said, "Simon, son of John, do you truly *agapas* me?"
> He answered, "Yes, Lord, you know that I *philo* you."
> Jesus said, "Take care of my sheep."
> The third time he said to him, "Simon, son of John, do you *phileis* me?"
> Peter was hurt because Jesus asked him the third time, "Do you *phileis* me?" He said, "Lord, you know all things; you know that I *philo* you."
> Jesus said, "Feed my sheep."

Jesus may have been assuming the "worst," therefore going for the "bottom line" contract. Peter's pain may have come from seeing it took so much to convince Jesus that a special affection still existed between them. But all of this does help us to see that *agape* is that final loyalty that holds on when all other reasons for affection seem to have disappeared.

"I sat for most of the afternoon of our anniversary," writes one of our friends who for ten years has watched the encroaching disability of his wife's dread disease of the brain. "I held Mary's hand. It was forty-nine years ago that day that we were married but today Mary showed no sign that she recognized me. She is merely passive now. Six months ago, I was the only one who could bathe her. She was terrified to be here in the rest home, and would not allow anyone to put her in the tub. Only me. I tell her that I will be back tomorrow, but her eyes seem glazed. But I will be back."

Job cried out during his great testing by Satan. "Though God slay me, yet will I trust him." There is a blind commitment in *agape* love. When one has chosen, the choice is irrevocable. It is, no doubt, the combination of these many facets of love: *eros, philia, storge,* and *agape,* which makes the mysterious marital bond virtually indestructible.

Enveloped by Love

What I hope you sense by now is that love is many splendored. It is too simple to say, "Agape is all that matters." I have wanted to illustrate the comprehensive bond which the four loves are able to form.

Eros alone cannot survive time and trouble, but it might do very well if it is buttressed by *storge* or *philia,* or by both. I suspect that it is only *agape* that can hold on alone in the face of the frosty winds of desolation and death. But that is a negative view. The more profound insight is that

every intimate marriage tends to keep all four loves alive and working so long as health and mental capacity are present. A good marriage might survive without the magic of *eros*, but it would be a pity that the excitement was gone. And partners who "drift apart" in their interests might still stand separate as pillars in the temple, but be held by *eros*, *storge*, and *agape*. We are all endowed with the instinct to do "parenting" with everyone who comes close to us, so the *storge* impulse might be expected to be virtually indestructible. And *agape* is a choice, so its targeted affection is the human equivalent of God's "steadfast love."

In this chapter I have wanted you to tiptoe around the mystery of human bonding. While the "four loves" are merely a partial set of lenses through which to examine the attachments that develop between people, they at least deliver us from the nonsense that "love" is simply a feeling. At the same time, it is also clear that we know very little about how magnificently God has created us—and with profound capacities for bonding.

QUESTIONS PEOPLE ASK

Q: I worry when you suggest there is something good about "eros." Isn't that what is meant by "infatuation"? And isn't the "high school crush" just another version of this heady stuff that messes up real love?

A: *Eros* alone is never enough, but any love without *eros* may seem like a lot of hard work with no magic in it. "Infatuation" is a helpful term if by it we wish to refer to the instant "falling in love" with someone too far away or impossibly remote from reality. I recall Billy Robinson from my high school days. He took his date to see some romantic movie in the forties, and he exclaimed that he was really in love with the star actress in the movie—whereupon his date told him never to call her for a date again. Both were silly responses. He cannot be "in love" with a star. And Billy's date was as far from reality as he was to let his silliness break their friendship. The "crush" has the same ingredients in it: the adored object of *eros* likely doesn't even know of the love affair. It is one-sided. It may span generations, as when one falls in love with the mentor: a teacher, a coach, or the boss. But the crush may disguise itself as "dependency" and fake helplessness to get the mentor into a "helper" role, only then to find that *eros* is unleashed. That is a formula for serious trouble. So, you are right. *Eros* alone is, indeed, a little crazy. But keep in mind that Ortega y Gasset is also right, a little *eros* in your tank can keep your love affair cranking right into the millenium.

Q: What if a bond is fading, or maybe it never was as strong as it might have been? What should we do?
A: I think Tevye was right in *Fiddler on the Roof*. "My father and my mother said we'd learn to love each other." Most of human history has seen parents selecting the partners for their young adult children. It was a fairly efficient model, and there were virtually no problems with teenaged intimacies, pregnancies, elopements, or suicides. So, if the old theory was right, then any two healthy people might be expected to find some magic in their relationship. Be sure to read the detailed description of the "pair bonding steps" in *Bonding: Relationships in the Image of God.* Then, the general diagnostic procedure I recommend is simply: (1) Identify the steps that may have been missed the first time around. (2) Evaluate whether those omitted steps have been "back-filled" after the consummation of genital intimacy. Then (3) begin to reinforce and strengthen the bond by going back to the weak point in the development and putting your intimate investment to work on the missed or weak points. Remember, finally, that (4) a healthy pair bond will be one in which all steps are continuously re-played, with a mild excitement which connects the present to your entire intimate history together.

Q: I like the "four loves" kind of bond you describe. Does it apply to parent-child bonding, too? And what happens if we missed the now famous "two-and-one-half hours" you and others recommend immediately after birth?
A: *Eros* as "adoration" applies to children, of course, and with healthy people, it never becomes sexual. But it is this adoration of parents and of children which almost literally

"glues" them to each other: visual bonding, with its accompanying touch. It is easy to see *philia, storge,* and *agape* in parent-child relationships, so, yes, all bonding seems to have significant common features. As to "making up for lost birth bonding," the principle applies everywhere the same, I think: Do not weep for what cannot be changed, and make up now by intentionally making the gestures of bonding, and let the feelings follow behavior, as they tend so faithfully to do.

Q: It seems you are saying that the "four loves" appear in patterns of eros, philia, storge, agape, *in that order. Is this the ideal, or is it virtually universal, something like the "bonding stages"? And do these need to be tended or "rehearsed" as the bonding steps throughout life?*

A: What an interesting question. Think of intimate relationships you have known. Do they follow a pattern of development? We have a "romantic ideal" of love "at first sight," and this is likely *eros.* But many of the best marriages picked up "common interests." They met in a laboratory, or in a social work placement: their *philia* interests became a shared vision. *Eros* came later. The *storge*-based friendships that sometimes led to marriage seem to me to have been "symbiotic" and flawed for long-term endearment. By symbiotic, I mean that one person "parented" the other as rescuer or care-giver, which care led to an intimate dependency pattern. This relationship in which one person is fulfilled by giving care and the other by receiving care is less than healthy in its beginnings. But *agape* love, since it is intentional positive regard, may precede all other loves and may also last when even life is gone. *Agape* love is a choice, and it is extended without feeling to large numbers of people. We could hope that mature people begin with *agape,* even before the lights of *eros* and *philia* come on. I expect that any sequence is fine. But you are right. All four loves need to be attended to, lifelong, in a healthy and growing love relationship.

Q: At church I hear so much about agape *being the highest love. Is there a biblical basis for the others? Is* agape *actually "better"?*

A: Jesus recognized the strength of *storge* love when he placed the call to obedient discipleship above the parental bond. And he placed it above the marital bond, too. This would suggest that *eros* and *storge* are implied and brought under the scrutiny of "targeted affection" in *agape* love. A marriage which had only *agape* holding it together might be safe, but it would lack the warmth which an intimate relationship might have known. I think I want to hold out for a fully orbed set of loves: a "four pack" of them.

Q: *You deal with moral development research theory. Are the 4 loves a "ladder" across the moral development levels?*
A: Ten years ago I thought perhaps they correlated with stages and levels. I now see that each of the four loves has a structural level appropriate to each of the levels and stages. *Eros* is not, essentially, self-centered, and *agape* is not, consistently, driven by high and holy ideals which match Kohlberg's Level C. Instead, *eros* may be directed to the adoration of the holy and the Wholly Other. And *agape* may be "targeted affection" determined to "have my own way," to "do it my way." I illustrate these extremes in *Bonding: Relationships in the Image of God.*

Eros may serve "self," or "others," or take the form of commitment to the worth of any person or value, including the strict adherence to expressing that adoration and fidelity. Each of the three levels of Piaget/Kohlberg is thus within the field: Level A is "egocentric," Level B is "hetero-centric"—other focused; and Level C is "etho-centric," committed to principled restraint and protection.

In the same way, *philia* may be focused on making friendships which benefit the self, or may be an "exchange" at a reciprocal level denoting concern for others. Yet *philia* often moves into Level C as the pure devotion to the memory of a past useful friendship.

Agape, of course, includes the highest, most pure form of intentional and unconditional commitment to a person or a value. But it also shows up as "intentional contracting" with others in reciprocal relationship. And, tragically, a person may even descend to Level A's egocentrism, declaring, "I want what I want when I want it."

2

Naked and Unashamed: The Universal Human Yearning

△

Bill and Betty were seniors in high school, both seventeen. Bill was quarterback on the varsity football team, and Betty was runner-up in the traditional "queen" contest at Homecoming. They were key officers in their church youth group, and both came from reputable families in their distinctly evangelical church.

When I asked the two of them how Betty's pregnancy happened near the end of that senior year—now eight years ago—they weren't quite sure. "We had been dating for two years. One thing led to another," Bill said. "I remember thinking sometimes that this must be wrong to be so intimate. But Betty really knew me and I trusted her. We completely undressed each other one afternoon, and I was amazed that I didn't feel guilty. We had both been raised right, so we knew we should be married to be doing this. We were terribly ignorant, but I think we trusted each other as much then as if we had been married. In fact, it was that trust that really 'stuck' when we discovered that we got a pregnancy the very first time we had intercourse."

It was Betty who had asked if she could see me for an hour. I was leading a couples' retreat as I do so often, and my afternoons were available for conference time. We sat down and Betty began to cry as the story of her pregnancy unfolded.

"We were so young, and we didn't know what we were doing. It all happened so fast—the first time we had intercourse and then the abortion was over almost before we knew what we had done. We were so ashamed. Our parents never knew. We kept the secret just between the two of us all these years. And I'm not sure that it hurts Bill as much as it does me. He doesn't talk with me about it at all."

"I want to talk to Bill," I interrupted.

"There he goes now," she said, pointing out the window of the screened porch where we were sitting.

As he stepped through the door, I said, "We are talking about the abortion."

"I know."

"Tell me, what effect has it had on you? Betty has described how it haunts her." Then Bill began to cry lightly and unloaded almost the same exact words—how young and naive they had been, how terrible had been the abortion decision, and how their two children were living reminders of their lost baby.

Then, after forty-five minutes of tears, I sat there holding the Olan Mills wallet photo of their two gorgeous children. And I wept with them. Finally, I returned the picture and reached for a hand from each of them. We sat there in our tiny circle. "Look at me," I said. "I want to tell you on the authority of the words of Jesus in John 20 that your sins are forgiven:[1] the bad timing of your sexual intimacy, the tragedy of the abortion. Now leave your guilt and shame with me."

"Do you work in your church?" I asked, and learned that they were co-teachers in a primary age class. "Watch for your chance to work in the teen division," I said. "One of the marks of your grief will be that you will have a message tattooed right on your forehead. It will say 'Betty and Bill are more than conquerors!' and you will be surprised that young people who are caught in the same pressures that swamped you will say to you, 'I don't know why, but I think I can trust you. Can I tell you something?' Then you will hear your story over and over in only slightly different terms. And Jesus will be equipping you to say, 'In the name of Jesus, I want you to know you are forgiven. This isn't the end of your life; it is just the beginning!' "

Yearning to Be Loved

Last week Justin, Lesli, and Heather, with their parents, Mike and Dorian, spent three hours watching their cat deliver her first litter of kittens—four of them. We heard the story in vivid detail. Each kitten arrived in a tubelike placenta, which the mother carefully broke away by licking with her tongue. She ate the covering, all the while carefully cleaning every square centimeter of the baby. The mother cat had about a half-hour to devote to each kitten before the next arrived. It would be easy to watch such a drama, as I did many times as a child on the Kansas farm, and imagine that the mother is simply "cleaning" the newborn. What we now know is that she is actually stimulating the newborn and communicating encouragement to it.

We have come late to look at human birthing behaviors and, in fact, in the modern "safe and painless childbirth" fads of the mid-twentieth century our medical scientists tried to so sedate the mother that she was immobilized for the entire birthing process. It turns out that human babies tend to fail and the mortality rate soars when infants are not cuddled, touched, and talked to.

By some reports the infant mortality rate during the first year of life was running above 50 percent in North America in the early 1900s. The babies were dying of a disease called *marasmus*. It was Dr. Henry Chapin, a New York pediatrician, who studied babies in "foundling homes" for orphans. In some of those homes the mortality rate during the first year of life consistently ran close to 100 percent! He found sanitary conditions, but the infants were being treated "scientifically." The attendants were following the newest child-rearing faddist: Dr. Emmett Holt, Sr., professor of pediatrics at Columbia University. In his 1894 bestseller, *The Care and Feeding of Children*, he advised parents on prenatal and early childhood care. Amazingly, the doctor urged parents not to rock or pamper their babies, to refuse to pick them up if they cried, and to feed them on schedule, preferably from a mechanically held bottle, so as not to addict the children to human touch and thus spoil them. The final edition of Dr. Holt's infamous book was dated 1935.

It is not only children who thrive when they are touched—all of us do! Lovers go for the skin, of course, and must sense the "health" of being valued. But we go for skin, too. Our handshakes extend the most dangerous and the most sensitive instruments of intimacy. We may use our hands to strike, hit, and bloody another person—one reason why parental discipline which uses the hand must be driven by love and not rage. But we also extend our hands to exchange skin contact with new friends, even strangers, if we are under social protocol which authorizes such touch.

With 800 graduate students milling through our halls, I keep my intraverted self mainly behind the doors of my office and my classroom. But I must occasionally sally forth to the campus post office or the Xerox room. I speak to almost no one except people with whom I have some significant personal or academic connection. On a recent occasion, I slipped through the maze, noticed Marty engaged in conversation, touched his forearm, whispered his name, and went on. A week later Marty and his wife Ann were in our home for the first of a series of couples' meetings we hosted on Wednesday nights as a "support group." When each person stated hopes and agenda items for the semester, Marty took the occasion to reconstruct the hallway incident. I was amazed. I had almost no memory of having touched him.

"I would do something like that," I said.

"You have no idea what it did to me. I can't remember how long it has been since someone other than Ann touched me in a way that I knew meant that I was respected and cared for."

Families develop rituals of touch which "charge the batteries" on a daily basis. My dad, who dragged me to the milking barn in the dark when I was five or six years old, did it because he thrives on having partners with him at work. He still needs working companions to gear up his energy. And I suppose at the time I was flattered at being thought of as a man, notwithstanding the fact that I was so short that I could not keep a three-gallon bucket of milk, even half-full, from dragging on the ground. But I remember my dad's gestures of affection. They consisted of fairly rough contact: the flat side of his foot into the seat of my pants, a fist playfully socked against my shoulder, or a slap on the back sometimes sharp enough to take my breath away. The verbal play, a literal nonstop chatter while hand-milking a dozen cows, assured me that nothing could ever come between my father and me, and that any exchanges, even in rebuke or discipline, would be grounded in his deep commitment to me and his delight that I was his son.

Yet, I cannot recall actual "formal" affectional behavior toward me. When, at thirty-five or so, I decided to embrace him as I was embracing my young teen-aged sons, I thought I had hugged an ironing board. Hugging was simply not something my dad used with other men. I had seen him wrestle with his brothers, chasing them in borderline violence around the farmstead. And I had been the privileged "firstling" of grandchildren to line up on the rim of the giant concrete water storage tank for the afternoon "skinny dip" with my dad, his father, and his four brothers. It was a storage tank for animal drinking water, freshly pumped by windmill from deep underground, and was always cold enough to turn you blue, even on 100-degree days. With all of this skin, and with the deep family ties, the males in the clan had to resort to playful touch; there would have been too much ambiguity had they embraced. There was hugging, of course, at the graveside when Dad's brother Irvin drowned in the Solomon River near Salina, shortly after his marriage. My grandfather held his daughters on his lap, teased them, and consoled them with fatherly ease, but the boys had to get their touching in other, more manly ways.

My mother's brothers were reared by warm, affectionate parents who absolutely bridled their physical gesturing. One of the senior cousins on the Royer side told me recently that his father confided our Granddad's parting advice on parenting:

"You will love your children, of course," Grandpa Royer

had told my cousin's father at the time of his marriage and leaving home, "but you must never let them know how much you care. If they knew, then you would never be able to discipline them properly, so just keep it to yourself."

The advice, happily, died with that final transmission, and most of us have been fortunate to be able to do our parenting in a tradition of honesty and affirmation, undergirded by unconditional love. I cite this history to illustrate how at variance it is with southern European patterns of hugging, kissing, and cheek-to-cheek embrace. But I share it also to show how infallibly a child is able to interpret the deeper meaning behind playful teasing, chasing, scuffling, and hitting.

Shame: Why Am I Afraid?

Infants show no shame. It would be easy to believe that shame is learned, except that it shows up universally when a child chooses—for whatever reason—to deceive. With deception, eye contact tends to be interrupted, since honesty gleams from the eyes. Adults who have something to hide sometimes use colored lenses to deal with their sense of embarrassment. I suspect that heavy use of facial make-up tends to correlate with shame. The "Jezebel" label was once used to describe women who hid behind too much make-up. And there may, indeed, be some correlation between the plastered coverings of some of our so-called "beautiful people" and Jezebel's efforts to hide the real hurt, "mileage," and grief. The bloodthirsty and jealous woman may have been overdoing her mascara and color toning for the same reasons people sometimes do today: they have to create a moving "blind" behind which to crawl to mend their broken and breaking hearts. It would be ironic, of course, if we were to discover that what appears to be "sexual signalling" were, instead, inadvertent advertising of mourning, grief, or shame.

"Where are you?" is the plaintive cry of God when the first man and woman sinned.

Then the man and the woman heard the sound of the Lord God as he was walking in the garden in the cool of the day,

and they hid from the Lord God among the trees of the garden.
But the Lord God called to the man, "Where are you?"

He answered, "I heard you in the garden, and I was afraid
because I was naked; so I hid."

Genesis 3:8–10

When I work with families and couples in trouble, I watch
their eyes. If they look directly into each other's faces when
they talk, I know there is hope. It indicates that we are
working with truth, however distorted it may be to suit
the speakers. But I shudder when I find people who will
not allow their eyes to "engage" when they are speaking
to each other. The original sin surely illustrates the breakdown of trust and the rise of deception. And we may need
no surer genetic connection to our first parents than to
acknowledge that we, like they, fall into shame when we
abandon trust and honesty.

The One-Flesh Magnet: God's Cure for Shame?

In Eden, the original magnet which re-united the "two
parts of the Adam" was innocent, virginal, "naked and unashamed":

So the Lord God caused the human to fall into a deep sleep;
and while the human was sleeping, God took one of the human's
ribs and closed up the place with flesh. Then the Lord God
made a woman from the rib he had taken out of the human,
and God brought her to the man. The man said,
"This is now bone of my bones
    and flesh of my flesh;
she shall be called 'Issha,'
    for she was taken out of 'Ish.'"
For this reason a man will leave his father and mother and
be united to his woman, and they will become one flesh.

The man and his woman were both naked, and they felt
no shame.[2]

Genesis 2:21–25

We miss the chief hallmark of the original nudity: innocence. We are so preoccupied with exploitation that clothing is essential if we are to be even relatively safe. We

have provided employment to millions in the garment and design industries—all because of our tendency toward deception and exploitation.

A young child may dart through the room naked, or even undress in the front yard, much to the consternation of parents but to the amusement of everyone else. We must have a racial memory of our own innocence and our laughter discloses a nostalgia to return to the carefree "way it used to be."

But soon enough we learn to undress behind closed doors, to pull the shades, and to demand privacy for our "naked" business. We know, as the fallen Adam knew, that we live in a booby-trapped world. We are not safe from others—or toward others, for that matter. Not safe, that is, until we find a person to whom we can open our hearts—share our secrets, be totally vulnerable.

The vision of the wedding night is that two people eager to be fully "known" by the other present themselves as gifts to the other. This is not "instrumental use" or even "instrumental exchange." It is the final surrender of all barriers, and willingness to be fully known by one other human being on earth. And "naked, unashamed" ultimately means precisely that: to risk everything into the care of a person we have come to trust based on slowly developed experience. We have "tested" the safety without even realizing we were doing it. I caution my spiritual formation groups, "Don't share anything here if you have any reluctance at all. Take very seriously the 'radar beep' that cautions you to check the faces for safety. Jesus warned us not to 'cast our pearls before swine'! And your pearls of suffering are the jewels around which grace can build great character."

Nudity, Pornography, and Exposure: Shameless Obscenity

I picked up a hitchhiker in the fall of 1973—the year many will long remember that university students were caught up in a craze of "streaking," bringing shocking nudity to many campuses. My young rider was leaving Lexington and heading north, as I did every week for two and a half years, toward Indianapolis.

"Have you heard of the streaking that has been going on at the University of Kentucky this week?" he asked me.

I had even seen some fleeting camera shots on local news, so I confirmed that I had, indeed, heard.

"Well, I did it once—Thursday."

Now this shy fellow who was huddling near his side of the cabin in the front seat of my Impala hardly seemed the type to be streaking.

"How did you get up enough nerve to do that?" I asked him.

"It was hard. But everybody who had done it kept saying it would give you a feeling like nothing else ever would."

"Were they right?

"It was different. I was scared to death."

The "streak," of course, is not displaying the "unashamed" part of our Creation formula. In fact, he was only technically exhibiting the "nakedness" side, given the speed and brevity of his circle around Patterson Towers.

I suspected then, as I do now, that when we see flirtations with nudity, we are observing one of the "marsupial hangovers" of our original innocence, a yearning for Eden, a desire to "know as we are known."

When a playwright works on the theme, as in the musical *Hair*,[3] we see additional dimensions. There the anesthesia of obscenity and vulgarity are added to the nudity. These are not bold and strong characters, but weak and wobbly people who must inject themselves with an identity "fix" before they are able to pull out the stops, take off the clothes, and find their way back to a replica of Eden where harmony, understanding, sympathy, and trust abound. The refrain climaxes with a hope that the sun will "shine"! The text of the songs calls for Eden, but imagines that it can be gotten by stoning ourselves out of our skulls until we can do the nudity trip in front of a capacity crowd. The Christian vision is that heaven will be the massed crowds of saints who have been delivered from their shame, and there they will "know as they are known," a symbol of virginal nakedness.

Let the Son shine! Let the Son shine!

"Nakedness" became a symbol of disgrace. Noah's sons found him both drunk and naked and approached him backward to cover his nakedness.[4] A man might put away his wife if he found some "indecency" in her, but the flaw was literally "nakedness," suggesting she was a promiscuous woman who could not "keep her clothes on."[5] And Jesus cited "fornication/harlotry" as a condition which might, indeed, mortally flaw a marriage,[6] perhaps using the condition as a parallel to that from Deuteronomy.

We have the distinction of living in an age of easy pornography. Skin photographs in magazines and movies abound, as do live sex shows in major cities on most continents.

If it is true that "Profanity is the lowest form of prayer," then pornography may be seen as the lowest form of intimacy. It may denote a hunger for honesty and openness which lies well beyond the reach of people who have hardened their minds and hearts to God and to other people. Yet they are "hooked" on the dream of nakedness without shame, so they shamelessly addict themselves to viewing other people's bodies, as if that in itself might satisfy the deepest hunger of the human: that of an intimate and exclusive relationship with one person who truly loves and respects.

Intimacy: The Acid Test?

Today I met Enrique. He is twenty-one, a student at Eastern Kentucky State University. His father kidnaped him from his mother in South America when Enrique was three. The tragic family, now divided between the two Americas, was gripped in poverty. Enrique's father stumbled into a church-supported child-care home not far from Richmond. There the boy grew up. At thirteen he began genital display to younger children. The authorities at the child-care facility were nonplussed. Enrique was a compliant child, he had been in the home for ten years. But his "skin hunger" appeared in a tragically deformed sexual behavior. The director of the center told me how he and his staff prayed for God to direct them to the right help. He made a phone call. "I can recommend just the right counselor," the Lexington pastor said, "Dr. William Cessna."

"Dr. Cessna, in only a few sessions, brought healing to Enrique," the director told me. "He was our miracle worker." The whole story moved me deeply, since Bill Cessna and I had been colleagues for more than ten years prior to his death, much of that time serving on the same faculty.

Voyeurism and rape are deformed cries for intimacy. Sometimes they are signs of the depraved appetite of the promiscuous person, but more often they have a deeper pathology. And often the behavior seems not to be grounded in what the rest of us would regard as "sexual motivation" at all, but in anger. In Enrique's case, his resentment at the loss and abandonment by his parents not only left him without models from which to learn the appropriate interpersonal graces which lead to intimacy, but he was also filled with rage. In therapy Dr. Cessna was able to let him release that anger, and to provide the gentle "mentoring" which affirmed his sexuality and helped him to learn the repertoire of skills necessary to move toward appropriate intimacy at an appropriate time. Dr. Cessna, missionary and Spirit-filled therapist, was able to bring more than therapy techniques to Enrique's case. Today Enrique is a mature, deeply committed Christian young man, and the director cites him as a living witness to the memory of a distinguished therapist whose career was cut short by a fatal illness at the age of fifty-four.

"Then Jacob said to Laban, 'Give me my wife. My time is completed, and I want to lie with her.'" So with these words, Laban permits the marriage. But Jacob is tricked and he awakens after the wedding night having married Rachel's older sister Leah. It is easy to speculate how well Jacob "knew" Rachel, if he didn't detect that he had the wrong woman until daylight! Perhaps it was a culture which prohibited voice contact, though Jacob had encountered Rachel alone at the well on his first arrival in Paddan Aram.[7]

My point is this: "to lie with" is an immature, instrumental motive for sexual intimacy. St. Paul advises, however, that "if they cannot control themselves, they should marry, for it is better to marry than to burn."[8] The peak of sexual "charge" for males today is at about age seventeen. The body's hormonal output crests then for about seven years before the slow descent. Size of external flaccid genitals enlarges during these years because of the high blood levels of androgens, especially testosterone. While the sexual appetite is psychologically shaped, the "motor" for finding some sexual expression is highest here. Daniel Levinson found in his famous study of forty men that without exception each established an intimate relationship with a woman during the "age twenty transition" which consisted of the years from seventeen to twenty-three. For these, he reported, they tended to marry in order to consummate "sexual intimacy." For those who waited until the age thirty transition, the motivation was for a life partner useful to the vocation. If the "young love" is driven by sexual desire, either from the male or the female, and if both are inexperienced, the long bonding process seems to set up a maturity in which neither demands to "lie with" the other in the instrumental sense. Mutual respect thrives between the young and the innocent.

The Hebrew word for "knowing" is used of the most mature sexual intimacy. But it is "knowing based on experience." Eating from the "tree of the knowledge of good and evil" set the stage for humans to move out in the long and painstaking search for meaning. What we might have handled by "instinct" seems to have moved to "knowing by experience," with all the pleasure, tedium, and risk involved. So, Adam "knew" Eve. Abraham "knew" Sarah. This was the painstaking "knowing by long experience." To "know" was sexual, of course, but it was a good deal more. And the pinnacle of sexual loving is detailed in the Song of Songs. Solomon presents the ballad of antiphonal songs between two lovers whose names suggest that they are the male and female sides of "one flesh personhood." Listen to some of the key lines:

Beloved

Let him kiss me with the kisses of his mouth—
for your love is more delightful than wine.

Pleasing is the fragrance of your perfumes;
   your name is like perfume poured out. . . .

Dark am I, yet lovely,
   O daughters of Jerusalem,
   dark like the tents of Kedar,
   like the tent curtains of Solomon.
Do not stare at me because I am dark,
   because I am darkened by the sun.
My mother's sons were angry with me
   and made me take care of the vineyards;
   my own vineyard I have neglected.
Tell me, you whom I love, where you graze your flock
   and where you rest your sheep at midday.
Why should I be like a veiled woman
   beside the flocks of your friends?

Lover

If you do not know, most beautiful of women,
   follow the tracks of the sheep
   and graze your young goats
   by the tents of the shepherds.
I liken you, my darling, to a mare
   harnessed to one of the chariots of Pharaoh.
Your cheeks are beautiful with earrings,
   your neck with strings of jewels.
We will make you earrings of gold,
   studded with silver. . . .

Beloved

Like an apple tree among the trees of the forest
   is my lover among the young men.
I delight to sit in his shade,
   and his fruit is sweet to my taste.
He has taken me to the banquet hall,
   and his banner over me is love.
Strengthen me with raisins,
   refresh me with apples,
   for I am faint with love.
His left arm is under my head,
   and his right arm embraces me. . . .

Lover

You are beautiful, my darling, as Tirzah,
   lovely as Jerusalem,
   majestic as troops with banners.

Turn your eyes from me;
  they overwhelm me.
Your hair is like a flock of goats
  descending from Gilead.
Your teeth are like a flock of sheep
  coming up from the washing.
Each has its twin,
  not one of them is alone.
Sixty queens there may be,
  and eighty concubines,
  and virgins beyond number;
But my dove, my perfect one, is unique,
  the only daughter of her mother,
  the favorite of the one who bore her.
The maidens saw her and called her blessed;
  the queens and concubines praised her. . . .

Lover

How beautiful your sandaled feet,
  O prince's daughter!
Your graceful legs are like jewels,
  the work of a craftsman's hands.
Your navel is a rounded goblet
  that never lacks blended wine.
Your waist is a mound of wheat
  encircled by lilies.
Your breasts are like two fawns,
  twins of a gazelle.
Your neck is like an ivory tower.
Your eyes are the pools of Heshbon
  by the gate of Bath Rabbim.
Your nose is like the tower of Lebanon
  looking toward Damascus.
Your head crowns you like Mount Carmel.
Your hair is like royal tapestry;
  the king is held captive by its tresses.
How beautiful you are and how pleasing,
  O love, with your delights!
                    Song of Songs 1:2, 5–10; 2:3–6; 6:4–9; 7:1–6

Today's love songs are hardly more explicit than this ancient and intimate exchange. If we smile at the strange
metaphors used to describe the naked body, we cannot say

that they do not evoke concrete images of power and strength. And all lovers know that when the "left arm" is under the lover's head and the "right hand" is embracing, then ultimate intimacy has arrived. But such intimacy belongs only to the lovers, and it must rest upon the absolute foundation of protection and trust. Every society has formulated a legal base as the minimum prior foundation for sexual intimacy: marriage. And where all are safe, the whole community applauds the privacy of the lovers.

In this chapter I have wanted you to see the urgent need all of us have to "tell it all" to some trusted companion. And I have wanted you to grieve with me, also, that what we call "cheap sex" in music and the movies is likely a cry for intimacy, however deformed and dangerous those signals are in a fragile civilization. I have wanted to join you or to ask you to join me in trying to sort out the beautiful from the tragic, but on balance, here as everywhere, God's Creation grace is more powerful than death and sin.

QUESTIONS PEOPLE ASK

Q: Do you approve of Betty and Bill having intercourse when they were unmarried seniors in high school?
A: Not at all. Nor would they want you to approve. They had suffered eight years of shame when I met them. Their "confessing" to me indicated their hunger to "come home to the truth"—the real meaning of the word repentance. But shame never repents until it is transformed into guilt. Guilt takes responsibility, then it takes steps to make things right and to be reconciled and to heal the past breach. I could wish that all high school people who have begun sexual intimacy had formed as strong a bond as Bill and Betty formed. They "formed one new person" of two who became one, and the cement of their sexual intimacy seemed actually to have been strengthened by the tragedy of their conspiracy to destroy the pregnancy. In this case, their deep grief had melted them together. But most young people do not consummate a well-bonded marriage with their original sexual partner. And few hold the bonding in absolute and sacred privacy, as they did.

Q: Are you saying that we can always blame a person's profanity or voyeurism or fascination with pornography on early childhood experiences, especially what parents do to children?

A: Many of my examples suggest that adult deformity is rooted in early childhood experience. But that is too simple, and you are right for stopping me cold to ask. The fact is, we cannot expect to find the roots of all deformity or sin in our family environment, since each person is free to choose, and each person experiences family, peers, and all of life "uniquely." No one else sees what a given person sees or constructs the same responses. And since "the heart of humans is evil, continually," there is a lot of grief in the world that is produced simply by evil. Scott Peck, in his *People of the Lie,* underscores for all of us that there is a psychiatric disorder which must be labeled "evil." It is different from neurosis or psychosis. At the same time, many people suffer skin hunger, fascination with nudity, and obscene ventilation of anger in clear connection to unfortunate early environment experiences. These people often find that psychotherapy or foundational faith experiences liberate them from the tyranny of past experiences. Almost always they have also to liberate the people who either violently or unintentionally were the instruments of their early trauma; they are enabled to forgive them.

Q: You sometimes seem to distinguish between "shame" and "guilt." How are they different?

A: I discovered the difference in my research on moral development.[9] The first level of moral reasoning is constructed with a view of "the self" at the center of the universe. The second level sees "the others' reality" as governing the universe and even the self. A third level places "universal values" above all governing entities and all "selves." Well, "shame" is distinctly the view of Level A. Shame consists of feelings of embarrassment, humiliation, and a host of narcissistic wounds. People suffering from shame confess nothing unless they are caught "red-handed." Then, they will tell only what has been spilled publicly. Shame does not set up a foundation on which repentance can occur. A person may pray to God and may seem to be "converted," but prayer to God when shame is the motor is prayer to "deliver me from this humiliation." Such religious expression is almost always followed by immediate abandonment of "faith," as things return to normal or they learn to cope with continuing shame with nonreligious tools.

"Guilt," on the other hand, has an enormous "social" dimension. Guilt takes responsibility for other people, for other people's expectations and hopes, and for people who have been hurt by irresponsible selfish behavior. Guilt is "other" concerned, which is typical of Level B of moral development. Guilt sets the stage for full confession. "You know what happened last week; well, that wasn't the first time. In fact, I need to ask you to help me make a list of all of the things I have shoplifted, because I am going to have to do something about it." Guilt evokes statements like, "I am a dangerous person. I hurt people. I have hurt you. And I don't want to keep on hurting people." I saw all of this being transformed in the conversation with Bill and Betty, and perhaps for the first time they were ready to "repent" and take responsibility for their past tragic failure. Such repentance linked with God's grace is the basis for the mystery of character transformation we call "conversion" or "the new birth."

3

Tragedy Comes in Two Colors:
Promiscuity and Double Bonding

△

Consider again the case of Bill and Betty, the high school
seniors who secretly got their abortion, then grieved for
eight years over the baby they had killed. They were
stabbed with loss and guilt every time they picked up their
two little children. "A boy and a girl," Betty told me as
she showed me their pictures. "Just what we had wanted.
And I know we killed a beautiful baby just like them. But
we were so young! We didn't know what we were doing.
We didn't ask anybody; nobody knew but us."

Today Bill and Betty are Sunday school teachers in the
same church in which they grew up. Their lives are high-
lighted by a long-term grief which has been marked by
forgiveness, and the mellowness they show is directly related to the way they faithfully supported each other across
the years of their guilt and grief. I alone have heard their
story, and in the privacy of their confidential telling, I was
suddenly aware that Jesus was authorizing me to tell them
their sins were forgiven.

Born Virgins

I recently made my every-semester appearance in a
high school classroom where a much-respected coach and

39

teacher gathers several classes and asks me to do a session on pair bonding. On my first invitation he cautioned me at the door that I would have to be very careful not to use religious, Christian, or Bible terms, since we had to observe the division between religion and public schools. I told him that my transparencies were full of crossover connections between science and the biblical vision.

"But I will be personally responsible for not offending any faith traditions here, or any non-faith ones, too," I said.

Now, at my most recent visit, the coach simply introduced me:

"Here's Dr. Joy. I invite him to come here every semester. Pay attention to what he says, he could save your life."

So on that visit, I simply presented the coach with an audio tape on pair bonding, walked on stage to the gigantic chalkboard, and wrote the word "VIRGIN" in large letters near the chalk tray in the middle of this twenty-foot-long board.

"I've got good news for you. You all started out as 'virgins.' And if you have escaped incest and sexual abuse, most of you still are."

Then, at the top of the chalkboard I drew double images of the male-female symbols, connecting them down to the word "virgin."

"And if you make it into that one exclusive, lifelong, intimate relationship each of you dreams of, you can still be a virgin: two persons become one flesh, naked and unashamed! Nobody ever lost virginity on the wedding night! To be a virgin is to be 'whole.' That's the really good news."

I went on, "But the bad news is that there are two powerful forces pulling on you. Both of them can pull with a lot of appeal. And either one of them can destroy your best dreams and leave you with a lifetime of pain and trouble."

Double Jeopardy Bonding

I moved to the right end of the chalkboard and wrote the word "Adultery."

"Let me check your vocabulary," I said. "What is 'adultery'? Can you define it?" I asked.

"Sex between married folks who aren't married to each other," was the response I got quickly.

"OK. But what does 'adultery' mean? Let me change it to 'adulterate.' What happens if somebody adulterates the Nicholasville water supply?"

"They put poison or something in it—they mix something else in so it's not the pure thing anymore."

"Exactly. So when one person gets adulterated by being intimate with two people, that's adultery," I said. "Now, before I get on with the bad things that can happen to you, let me tell you a story." And I told them the Bill and Betty story, the high school abortion, their marriage at nineteen, and their two beautiful children, all wound around with the tragic sense of losing their first baby.

"Did Bill and Betty commit adultery?" I asked.

"No, because they weren't married anyway. And they weren't 'adulterating' any bond to anybody else."

"Right. But let me complicate it," I went on. "Suppose that Bill cut out on Betty and let her go through the abortion alone, abandoned her, and got another girlfriend. Then, Betty gets married to someone else. And Bill marries another woman. Do we have adultery now?"

"Well, things are never going to be the same as if they hadn't had sex and the abortion," someone said. "It's sort of like something had died—something important and beautiful was gone forever."

"Did it die? Or does it become a sort of 'ghost' that is going to haunt the next intimate relationship, maybe lifelong?" I asked.

"More like that, I think. Neither one of them will ever forget. And maybe they will always think that they really were more in love with each other than anybody else, ever."

"So, has their bond been adulterated—spread too thin, diluted with other loves? If Bill's eyes mist over when he is with his wife and she asks him what he's thinking about, has his affection been adulterated? And if Betty sobs in the night and her husband learns about the high school sex and the abortion, will he sit up in bed and wish he could get hold of Bill for just five minutes to make him pay for messing up Betty's life?"

I turned to walk toward the other end of the chalkboard. "One way to lose your 'wholeness' is to make the gestures of love without protecting the relationship by legal marriage. Your parents may break you up. You may 'run away' from the heavy obligations which your intimacy creates. Or you may simply become frustrated by the fact that you cannot have each other now, for the rest of your lives. And any break-up is sure to set off the 'adulterating' effects for both of the people. Bad as it is, that tends to be the best of the options after the break-up of a bonded relationship."

The Promiscuity Trap

I walked to the left end of the chalkboard and wrote the word "FORNICATION." Then I turned to ask:

"Can you tell me what 'fornication' means? It isn't a word you hear every day around a high school."

"Sex between unmarried people."

"OK. Maybe. But I'm not sure that definition is helpful. I grew up thinking that is what it meant. The Scriptures of the Judeo-Christian tradition use the word in a very specific way, and it is not at all what the dictionary says it is. So if we take our popular definition to Scripture, it doesn't make much sense when we read it. I want to show you what it means historically, not what we use the term 'fornication' to denote today.

"Suppose Bill and Betty break up after intercourse, perhaps even before the pregnancy. Take the case further. Bill says to Betty out on a date, 'If you won't have sex with me, then this is our last date.' Now, I want to stress that this is not what happened in the case of Bill and Betty. And they did not break up. But when any person goes after sex for its own sake—to make points with one's friends, for example, or simply to feel the kicks of a new experience by getting a willing partner to cooperate, then sex becomes a 'commodity.' "

We get the word "pornography" from a Greek word, *porneia*, which means "sex as commodity." The same root word is translated in the Bible as harlot, prostitute, and whoremonger. Even the English word "prostitute" means "to degrade by using in a wrong and cheaper way." So a man may prostitute his inheritance by gambling it away. Or students may "prostitute" their semester in college by flirting with the drug scene, the singles' bars, or the all-night card games, until suddenly a whole vocation may evaporate before their eyes.

I went on to explain how "fornication" in the King James Bible consistently refers to promiscuous sexual predators and addicts. It was such a dangerous sexual orientation that Jesus is quoted as mentioning it in the famous teaching about divorce in Matthew 19:9. When two persons divorce who have been sexually bonded, the break-up leaves both of them in grief and if they remarry, they will carry the ghost of the previous lover into the new relationship. Jesus calls this "committing adultery" upon re-marriage. But if one of the marriage partners is a "fornicator," then there may be no ghost to haunt a future marriage. Sexual addicts who use people as objects tend to destroy the bond before it is established. So there may be no "adultery" to haunt a future bond. We will look at the words of Jesus on this subject a little later.

So under the word "FORNICATION" on the chalkboard, I wrote the Greek word *porneia*. And under it I wrote pornography, prostitute, whoremonger, and sexual addict.

FORNICATION	"Two become one flesh. . . ."	ADULTERY
	12	
	11	
	10	
"porneia"	9	"moicheia"
	8	
pornography	7	adulterate
prostitute/harlot	6	double bond
whoremonger/hustler	5	"ghost" bond
sexual addict	4	schizophrenic
promiscuity	3	bonding
	2	
	1	
	VIRGIN	

A *porneia* person, then, is a sex-a-holic—a sexual addict who uses sexual sensations as a sort of god, and doesn't care about people who may be used or hurt along the way. You can see how the sexual abuser, the incestuous parent or other adult, and much of masturbation may be falling into the *porneia* trap: sex for its own pleasure alone. It is not surprising that Jesus is quoted in Matthew 19:9 to the effect that "fornicators" who are married may so default on the marriage that at the time of divorce the other spouse may remarry without breaking or adulterating a bond at all. To be married to a "fornicator" would be to be always afraid the spouse would be "on the make" with another partner, and to know that there is no "one flesh" mind and spirit in the relationship at all.

Virgins, Fornicators, or Adulterers

"So, what about Bill and Betty? Would you say that they were guilty of fornication? We have decided that they did not adulterate each other's future bonds. They finally protected the original bond by marrying each other, unlike most people who are sexually intimate before marriage. Were they fornicators?"

"Well, not by your definition they weren't. They weren't sexual addicts. They were innocent. But they got there too soon."

"Thanks. I wanted you to wrestle with the real issues. You are right. According to most dictionaries, they are guilty of fornication. But for people who study the Bible it is not so clear in the historical use of the words. The Greek and Hebrew words which are translated fornication and fornicator also come into English as harlot, prostitute, and whoremonger. And the consistent use in both Old and New Testaments is of sexual aberration and addiction. We use the word promiscuous to denote a person who seems never to be sexually satisfied and is constantly 'on the make,' using first one, then another person."

With fornication and adultery defined, I went to the middle of the chalkboard where I had begun. Above the word virgin and below the two interlocked male-female symbols, I drew a messy circle. It was still on the lifelong virgin trajectory, but it was in trouble. I went on:

"The timing was terrible," I said. "Bill and Betty are among the very few lucky ones. They were so absolutely faithful to each other that they never told one person about their intimacy. Most of Bill's friends drop the whole thing in the locker room, or to best friends at least, to brag on their 'scoring.' When they do that, they have taken the plunge into *porneia* with its tendency toward serial sex partners, one-night stands, and promiscuity even after marriage.

"Bill and Betty had to wait until they could swing the marriage and they endured an enormous test on their young love. When a bond is sealed, it deserves to have daily maintenance and public affirmation of the 'one flesh' that is a secret reality. But they survived, got to the marriage altar still with their precious bond intact, and today have a healthy and strong marriage which has been tested by fire!"

Premarital Sex: What Kind of Sin?

So in the fuzzy circle I drew there, I wrote "Tragic Timing." And I went on to explain that they had taken terrible risks with themselves and with each other. They ran the risk of falling off the virginal trajectory into future damage to other marital bonds—"adulterating" each other's future marriages. Or, I said, they might have rebounded into sexual promiscuity as they set off a series of one-night stands and casual *porneia* addictions. But in their amazing story, Bill and Betty managed to save everything except their first baby. And they are carrying that grief for the rest of their lives.

Remember that "promiscuity" or "fornication" would have been an easy trap for Bill or Betty. If either of them had bragged to friends about their sexual experience, they would have "reduced the other to a mere object," hence fornication. And if Betty had had the abortion and if Betty or Bill had leaked that information to anyone, Betty would have been a potential target of predator males, and her shattered sense of self might easily have heightened her vulnerability to almost any kind of male who would give her attention.

As tragic as premarital intimacy is, it often falls somewhere other than in the *porneia*/fornication category. And such intimacy is not *at the time* a violation of another bond, or adultery. The interpersonal failure (remember the last six of the Ten Commandments regulate "interpersonal relationships," while the first four regulate human-God relationships) or sin of premarital intimacy boils down to two tragedies: (1) lack of respect for the self and the other person, in terms of long-range emotional health; and (2) defrauding one another—making the gestures of full trust without guaranteeing through social/legal protocol that such trust was indeed merited. The question always remains for those of us who defrauded a partner before marriage: If I lost control of my sexual impulses and could not wait to arrange the legal protection we both deserved, am I served notice that I am vulnerable to some future moment of weakness or passion which comes from a nonmarital "opportunity"?

How Promiscuity and Double Bonding Differ

We have looked, now, at two traditional terms: fornication and adultery. It is clear that both are destructive. They damage both the person who initiates the sexual contact and the person who responds or is "used." Beyond this, of course, like concentric circles of people who are damaged, immediate affectional ties to spouses, children, parents, and ultimately every human being are damaged when any person slips into deformed sexual behavior and relationships.

I have wanted you to be able to discriminate between popular uses of fornication and adultery. Let me summarize:

In popular use, adultery refers to sexual contact between persons who are married to other partners. We have even come to say that if just one of the partners in an illicit pair is married, it constitutes adultery. *But in historical use, adultery refers to the weakening of any healthy bond by the intrusion of an alien bond into the previous exclusive relationship.* So our young are appropriately anxious not to intrude on a "going steady" relation because they instinctually know when two people "belong to each other." It is a healthy sign when everybody drops back and punts when two of our young "pair off" at school. "Dating around" is rejected by many people of all ages because the yearning for one exclusive relationship is so strong. Absolute respect for a developing bond is the healthy sign in romantic behavior; the opposite and deformed sign is the trivial, "consumer," explorer, adulterating pattern.

In popular use, fornication refers to sexual intercourse between unmarried partners. *But in historical and biblical use, fornication refers to sexual predators who have only instrumental regard for their sex objects.* They may be "nice" in order to use the person, but they tend to quickly abandon or simply offer to "pay for the abortion" and to split. Pornography, grounded in the same Greek root as fornication, is similarly, "graphic sex for kicks." When you lay down three dollars for a *Playboy* magazine, you have not only made your instrumental exchange in support of Hugh Hefner's empire, but you have named your own price: "I am a three-dollar piece of flesh." The "porn" issue cuts both ways.

"Instrumental exchange" denotes a kind of "reciprocal deal," in which a "swap" or trade is made. "You scratch my back and I'll scratch yours," is the oldest idiom of instrumental exchange. And fornication/pornography is the classical "instrumental exchange." Sex for money. Favors for care. You can extend the list. Perhaps the reciprocal "deal" is nowhere clearer than in that amazing and ancient poster in the Book of Proverbs:

PROMISCUITY	[ONE FLESH VIRGIN]	ADULTERY
The		but the
prostitute		adulteress
reduces		stalks
you		your
to a loaf		very
of bread . . .	[Exclusive Bond]	life.
	Proverbs 6:26	

It is easy to ignore the first line because not many people use prostitutes. But remember that "fornicate" and "pornography" widen our understanding. So read it these ways, too:

The fast boyfriend reduces you to a mere piece of flesh.
The fast girlfriend reduces you to a Big Mac and a Coke.
The X-rated movie reduces you to a mass of quivering flesh.
The *Playboy* reduces you to a masturbating animal.
The guy with the hot car seduces you with marijuana!

The key in all of these is the phrase "reduces you." That is, the reduction cuts both ways, always. It is the great leveler in every way. We reveal our own true value by the price we put on other people or objects we use for sexual satisfaction. This is no doubt because of the fact that our sexual identity is the core of our self, the definition of the heart of our being.

Contrast this "reduction of the self to a mere thing" with the old wedding vows: "With all my earthly goods I thee endow!" Or consider St. Paul: "Don't you men know that your bodies belong to your wives; don't you wives know that your bodies belong to your husbands?"[1] And here is a profound distinction between fornication and exclusive love: *Fornication makes "deals" for sexual pleasure. Exclusive bonding finds a way to transfer complete ownership of everything one is and hopes to be into the hands of the other.* Marriage is the legal way that all of one's person and property are fully received and owned by the spouse.

So here is the tragedy of promiscuity. Since our sexual identity is at the core of our being, we cannot waste it, spread it around. We can only fuse it with one other exclusive person to form one whole human: the one-flesh union which we protect in every society with public marriage. So look at the Proverb again:

The prostitute reduces you to a loaf of bread,
but the adulteress stalks your very life.

Sexual addicts—the playboys, playgirls, harlots, and whoremongers—have blunted their bonding ability and have confused their memories. Homosexual addicts and promiscuous women tell the same story: "For a while I wanted to know only their first names. But finally, I would tell them I didn't even want to know any kind of a name. I could pretend better without any point of reference for my memory."

But adultery is another story altogether. Adultery is not promiscuity; it is schizophrenic bonding. The limited fabric of one person's "one-flesh" bond is stretched until it rips; it simply cannot cover a double bond. So the adulteress "stalks your very life." But in our time, we certainly have to read that line in other ways, too:

The boss who seduces you will stalk your very life.

The secretary who invites you to the secret rendezvous threatens to end life on this planet as you have known it.

The "best friend" who offers to comfort you will haunt you for all your life.

Say it any way you need to. Respect-based friendships turn into love affairs if sufficient bonding time is invested— for any reason whatever. And sexual intimacy, however innocent it may seem, will establish first and worst as a competing adversary to your original and perhaps legally protected bond. At the best, it will remain a secret and indelible "ghost" forever turned loose to haunt your first love.

Some Paths to Promiscuity

Any sexual appetite that is shaped and fed by "sex objects" which are "used" and abandoned, will throw us off the royal road to sexual fulfillment and lifelong "one-flesh" innocence. These include:

Masturbation based on stimulation derived from pictures, memories of movies, videos, music, poetry, and the like. This tends to be *porneia*. In contrast, masturbation based on the frustration of "having to wait until I can protect the relationship with public marriage" to a beloved and real person may be grounded in respect and responsible restraint. So not all masturbation is necessarily of the "fornication" type.

Dating for sexual kicks is always fornication, whether or not intercourse occurs. Jim confessed, when trying to get ready for marriage, that he had never in his life masturbated. "I could always get a girl to do it for me." Jim took what I thought was rather silly pride in still being a "virgin." He didn't know what a virgin was, just as he didn't realize he had been fornicating since fourteen. I regret to tell you that his marriage failed and it is unlikely that he will find the necessary glue for a lasting relationship; he has become sexually addicted. He "uses" people for sex, always on his own terms.

Intercourse to "score" is always fornication, and the "third-rate romance" in a "low-rent rendezvous" is obviously not leading anywhere other than to sexual promiscuity.

Negotiated intercourse, by which one of the partners makes sexual action the price to be paid if the relationship is to continue, is clearly "fornication," because it has reduced the partner to a mere object to be used. So, when Alice broke her engagement because Frank demanded intercourse before the marriage or threatened to break the engagement, she took him seriously and accepted the break-up.

Sex for money or food or survival is always stooping to fornication. A fourteen-year-old who appealed to a businessman for help said he was a runaway. "How do you survive?" the man asked him. He took him to his physician who examined the boy and found that he had been severely sexually assaulted. Asked about what was going on, he said, "I'm a hustler." He could get money for performing for other people. "What I'd really like," he told the businessman, "is to go home with you."[2]

Group sex is always fornication. Sexual intimacy is for privacy and "knowing as we are known" requires the absolute protection of the secrets shared.

Bragged sexual exploits are always fornication. When sexual "performance" is reported to a best friend or a locker room, the bond that might have been formed by the sexual contact is "prostituted" and wasted as it is dangled out in front of other people.

Forced exposure of sexual experience often tilts the victims toward *porneia*. When parents or other authority figures "make an example" of a couple by public exposure and humiliation, they may have themselves "caused the innocent to become fornicators" by displaying their untimely but otherwise healthy bonding process.

A *"rebound effect" after a break-up* tends to turn both partners toward promiscuity. If they start up another relationship to staunch their grief, they will tend to follow the same intimacy pattern into the new relationship, even with a naive partner. Most fornicating, promiscuous persons began with a nicely bonded experience which was unprotected by public marriage. And when it broke, they moved too quickly to another relationship which, for lack of slow pre-bonding stages, failed, and a whole string of promiscuous people have been spun off as waste from the pair of once-bonded lovers.

Beyond these, *incest, rape, sexual abuse,* and *exhibitionism* are consistently and tragically "fornication"—the use of other persons for sexual stimulation and egoistic pleasure.

Some Ways to Fall into Schizophrenic Bonding

Adultery can creep up on us from almost anywhere. Most often the encroaching alien bond develops in the work place, but any place will do.

Work colleagues are especially vulnerable to each other. Look again at the twelve bonding steps summarized in chapter 1. It is almost inevitable that any two people whose sexual magnets are healthy are vulnerable to sexual bonding if voice, eye, and occasional tactile/touch contact are occurring.

Two-couple friendships often set up the scenario in which one of the alien couples will pair off, typically leaving an odd couple which has not experienced the alien bonding effect. It is curious that three or more couples who form a social network almost never set the scene for an "adulterating" of one of the couple bonds, but two-couple sets are highly vulnerable, and the typical scene has the confidentiality shared so deeply that someone suggests "swapping" for harmless fun. But the adultery stalks the very life of people who step over the edge into those experiments.

Client-professional relationships have abundant soil in which an alien bond may grow. This is especially true of those confidential professions such as law, medicine, psychiatry, psychology, and pastoral care. In each of these, people with deep hurt and trouble place themselves in a professional relationship where they are assured of trust and confidentiality. And none of us is more vulnerable to sexual attraction than when dealing with deeply emotional material. If emotions of empathy, sympathy, and pity are aroused, they tend to be linked directly to sexual arousal, and over several hours of contact, an alien bond finds easy rootage. "I have never been really loved by my husband, and I have never experienced sexual climax since we were married five years ago" is a typical confidential confession. That confession has obvious overtones of seduction, as if to say, "But I think you are a good lover and you could bring me the pleasure my husband cannot bring me."

Some Strategies for Faithfulness to the One-Flesh Vision

Chapters 5 and 6 explore how some people have recovered from promiscuity (*porneia*) and how others have recovered from double bonding (adultery or *moicheia*). So at this point I want to talk about prevention, not cure or recovery.

1. *Nourish the virginal dream.* Innocence is "standard equipment on all models." Young children easily identify sexual differences and easily pick up a sense of privacy where family relationships are healthy, spontaneous, and respect-based. Well before the onset of pubescence, children want to be respected and given privacy. Paul Tournier insists that this sense of privacy is an important foundation for "individuality." Those "secrets" held within the self become the base, then, for "personhood" that consists of "sharing one's secrets." The "naked and unashamed" phenomenon of intimate sexual contact is the ultimate disclosure of secrets. Except where children have been sexually abused or where they have been given no privacy, the

virginal dream of ultimate sharing with one other person, alone, in one lifetime, is also "standard equipment." In this way, every generation starts over, no matter how corrupted previous generations have become.

Families contribute to the virginal dream which includes exclusive, legally protected, sexual union with one exclusive person of the opposite sex. They do it in at least these ways:

2. *Support childhood "sweetheart" expressions.* Last week as we held tickets to see Walt Disney's *Fantasia*, with three grandchildren in tow, Jason, now ten, came bounding into the mall with unbridled excitement.

"Can you believe this?" he exploded in a whispered shriek. "Kristin, my girlfriend, is here to see the movie!"

"You've got to introduce us, remember. We haven't met her," I gurgled back in matched enthusiasm, I expect.

But it was not to be. Jason, at ten, lacks the social skills that handle formal introductions across the generations. I could see he was restless. "Here is your ticket," I said, tearing the five tickets apart. "If you want to sit with her and her mother, that will be fine."

Imagine our surprise fifteen minutes later as we slipped in with a pair of our older children, to find that Jason had seated himself in a row, alone, directly behind Kristin and her mother. He was not yet ready for "sitting with your girlfriend" at a movie. Yet his excitement at finding Kristin and her mother at the movie would have suggested a much more intimate agenda was at work. But many adults, including parents, ridicule, laugh, and otherwise embarrass young impulses to "pair off." In one of the most painful cases I have worked with, parents mocked the young boy's romantic impulses, made fun of him for being interested in girls, and triggered an amazing impulse to instrumental sex— the hidden, secret rendezvous of a massage parlor or a prostitute.

3. *Hold off "couple" dating.* Thank God for every opportunity your young adolescent has for "group dating" or "swarming" socially. Church and school activities which cluster youth without a "date" agenda provide the best settings in which the healthy monogamous "magnet" can find its signals. In the early teen years, when adult chauffers

are essential, the social development can proceed without social or sexual pressures to "keep up" or to "perform." Parties in homes need parental presence, support, and food management, with light surveillance to keep the environment free from really destructive experimentation. But these are the years free from intentional "couple dating," which might nicely be delayed until very late high school years, and then only on special occasions, with plenty of protocol, family participation, and celebration.

4. *Support "monogamous" dating.* I am amazed at the large numbers of conservative, fearful parents who insist that their teens and young adults "date around." They have not contemplated that if a maturing person could do that, they would likely be showing symptoms of a defective bonding ability. When John returned from Fort Collins and the week-long youth retreat long years ago, his first announcement to us was, "I've met the woman I'm going to marry." And almost in the same breath, he blurted out, "and I've got to go now and break the news to Vera."

We cringed. We had had Vera around the house on special occasions for two years. John, away in college, would make occasional weekend visits home to see her in the queen's court or other high moments in her sophomore year of high school. Now, in a flash, it ended. It took Robbie and me six months to get over the shock of letting go, but for John it was a moral imperative: he could not at the same moment be committed to one woman and deceiving another. Today's teens, with their earlier physiological/sexual development, are quite aware that dating is not just fun and games, it is lively seriousness, with full implications for future full intimacy. The old party games which rode on faked intimacy: spin the bottle, post office, last couple out, and a "Sadie Hawkins" date for an evening, are passé. Today's teens refuse to play at thinly disguised gestures which they know to be the prelude to full sexual union. They are possessed of a dream to share with one person, exclusively, for a lifetime.

5. *Focus on ultimate intimacy within marriage.* With the awakening of pubescence and the internal appetites for sexual expression, I like to encourage the junior high set

with a well-developed fantasy of the future. As I conclude the final session of a six-week sex education course, as I have done for several years for parents and pre-teens at Trinity Hill United Methodist Church, for example, I love to say to them: "I'm going to make you responsible for protecting each other for the next six years or so. You are your brothers' and your sisters' keepers. If you ever learn that anybody in this room is about to go out with someone you know is a sexual predator and is dangerous, I want you to promise now to go up to them and say, 'Hey! Do you know what kind of a person you are fooling around with? They're dangerous.'" Then, turning toward the pastor, I say, "Here is a man who will stand at the front of the church sometime within the next ten years and watch you come down the aisle or out of the side door to be married. He will be here to answer your questions and to help you make tough choices between now and then. And even if some tragedy occurs, he and the congregation will be here to put you back together."

I have found that sixth grade children already have made a decision about sexual experimentation. This is no new phenomenon, as much as we would like to blame the present culture for the hype in sexual pressure. It is rooted in the biology of adolescence. I do not know where the vision of sexual purity comes from, but I know that pre-teens are already deciding whether to wait for marriage or to do the *porneia* trip, just for kicks. At the very season of life when the fires that motivate sexual intimacy are hottest, the media and the entire popular culture seem bent on peddling experimentation, casual sex, and the entire smorgasbord of *porneia*.

6. *Bite the bullet, repent, and change.* On a Sunday morning recently, a fashionable woman in her thirties spoke to me in the narthex after I had appeared as the guest preacher. "I want to thank you for whatever it was that you said at the all-night retreat Friday night with the high school crowd here. Yesterday morning when David came home, he went to his room with grocery bags under his arm, and loaded up all of his *Playboy* and *Penthouse* magazines he has collected for a couple of years, and I watched

him burn them in the barbecue pit in the back yard." I had walked the teens through the "basic life intimacies" which comprise the heart of *Bonding: Relationships in the Image of God*. I had never attacked the popular pornography, but had cited famous playboys who are impotent at forty, and quoted Roger Staubach from his interview on nation-wide television. He was asked how it felt to compare himself with another popular quarterback known to be a playboy and who was so "sexually active." Roger coolly responded, "Well, I think I'm as sexually active as he is; the only difference is that all of mine is with one woman." So David went home and burned his *Playboys* and *Penthouses*. Ultimately the sexual choices are personal. So we do ourselves and our young a favor by putting the responsibility on them to make the moral choices they will be making anyway with or without our authorization.[3]

Not long ago a group of us sat around my mahogany conference table. We had been together for an hour each week for almost three years. Now, with three new members, we were rehearsing our "age twenty transition" event. Daniel Levinson's famous study of forty men[4] found that virtually all of his subjects had to deal with four things between ages seventeen and twenty-three: breaking away from home, attempting to establish intimacy with a woman, choosing a mentor, and catching a serious "life vision." We had worked through the details two years earlier, but in the review session, Mel summed up his efforts at intimacy:

"From the age of fifteen until I was in University, I took every girl I dated to bed. That went on till I was a sophomore at Tech. That was when I met Candy. Her dad was a Free Methodist minister in the city, and she wouldn't date me except to go to church. It was really frustrating. I had gone to church once in a while when I was sleeping with my girlfriends. I would feel so guilty, I'd sometimes put all the money I was carrying in the Sunday morning offering."

"Did it help?" I asked.

"Well, I felt a little better. But I always went back."

"Anyway, she wasn't about to let me have sex. But a funny thing happened. I was going to her dad's church all the time, and God got a hold on my life. I got saved.

So at the age of twenty, I became a virgin, and I didn't have sex again until our wedding night!"

A chuckle started around the room, then a quiet smile replaced the tendency to laugh. Mel was right. That was exactly what had happened. He became a virgin. And he still is—this innocent, honest, healthy man has proved again that the God who has created all things good, can make all things new through Jesus! St. Paul suggested the same thing when he listed off all of the bad things we could have been into, then turned the whole evil list around with "That is what some of you were" before Jesus transformed you by washing, sanctifying, and justifying grace.[5]

In this chapter I have asked you to do a bold thing: suspend your traditional definitions of fornication and adultery and try on the special lenses derived from Scripture use of the distinctions between the two. If you followed along with me, I brought you out with some lively commitments to sexual integrity, but you found them now grounded in larger, more carefully defined concepts. You are ready now to face the rather striking differences in the forms of hurt and damage that accompany fornication and that come with the territory of adultery. Chapters 5 and 6 unfold strategies for reconstruction of each.

QUESTIONS PEOPLE ASK

Q: So what you are saying, then—that when two people without previous sexual experience come together and form a bond, it may be a "virginal bond"? I always thought this was fornication.

A: You have a lot of company, and we often weep that people become sexually intimate without adequate acquaintance—they don't yet "know" each other in the larger global sense. But yes, the bond that forms together between them may very well be a "creation-based" bond—referred to by Jesus as "what God joins together." I was startled to find that the Old Testament has no rules to cover what happens when young, unbetrothed people become sexually intimate. Only sexual predators are addressed by Deuteronomy 22, not intimate and inexperienced young lovers. I conclude that this omission in Old Testament rules is very significant, and that it is likely missing because families always find a way to protect their young through immediate legal means, even though dowry and formal exchanges have to be arranged "after the fact."

Q: What would you call premarital intercourse between serious lovers, then, if it isn't fornication and it isn't adultery? There surely is a serious sin involved. Does it have any name at all?

A: I learned from a junior high fellow what the sin is called. It is "deception, fraud, and lying." After I had done a young teen version of a seminar on human sexuality, with its gentle constructions about "what it means to be a man and to be a woman," and had asked them to contract to be responsible for being "my brother's and my sister's keeper," Danny stayed behind.

"Do you remember the girl who was sitting right in front of you when we were sitting on the carpet in circles talking about what we like best about being a man or a woman?" He pointed to the spot on the floor in front of me.

"Only vaguely," I confessed.

"Well, last week we had this trip into Knoxville, you know, in the church vans. And on the way home, I sat on the back seat with her. And I don't think I will ever date her, or anything like that. But sitting there in the dark where nobody could see us, we sat close to each other, and we, well, we hugged and even kissed some, and it felt pretty good. But now when I see her, I feel like apologizing to her, because I feel like I lied to her or something. See, I didn't really mean all of what I was saying to her. I'm not going to take her out, even when I start dating."

"You've got a good conscience," I said. "And congratulations on taking it seriously. If I had a daughter, I could wish that she would find a friend like you. Always be sure that your gestures match your heart and your mind. Keep your feelings and the tough facts of real world responsibility tight together, and you will make it to the wedding on time, I guarantee you. It takes your whole life with nothing held back to carry through with total loving. Keep telling the truth and living the truth."

I find that nicely formed young people who have been well disciplined in their childhood, but not abused, tend to resist patterns of stealing, lying, cheating, and premarital experimentation. I take this to be a direct evidence of God's grace and image imprinted universally in the young where a father and a mother faithfully represent God's character through their care and discipline of the child. I discuss this, of course, in detail in the chapters on parenting in *Bonding: Relationships in the Image of God.* But the original sin has also left its mark. There is a central tendency to deceive, to defraud, and to exploit other people whenever it is to our advantage: the root of stealing, cheating, lying, and premarital sex. So it is critical that we not only give consistent care and discipline, but that we bring the children face to face with the need for interior honesty with themselves and with God.

The first accountability, of course, is between child and parent. "Coming home to the truth" as a foundation for discipline is rehearsal for the critical event of converting repentance. "To repent" is to come home to the truth. Adolescence is the season when most of our young must come to terms with God's call to honesty and integrity, and that call is nowhere more confrontive than when it is a call to sexual integrity. But we need to abandon "fornication/ promiscuity" as a label for young lovers who make bad judgments with bad timing. Most of them suffer enough grief over their real failures: miscalculating emotional anguish, and sensing guilt for allowing passion to justify potential fraud against each other and against the self as well.

Q: I am a pastor, and now that you have defined "fornication" as promiscuity instead of just "premarital sex," you have helped me to clarify a problem I have faced in the past. I now know that people who have been promiscuous make terrible marriage risks. Just now I am facing the issue of allowing a relatively innocent person to marry one with a track record which includes the "rape" of his best friend's virginal fiancée and impregnating her just before the wedding. He has a ten-year reputation for being a playboy. Should I intervene, and how?

A: That's really tough material! I have found that separate sessions are appropriate in premarital counseling, and one question I use is: "Do you have some idea of whether your fiancé has a track record of faithfulness in sexual matters?" Such a question opens a door for people who have wondered, but are not sure. And, depending on your credibility with them, you may have helped them to begin to predict fidelity after the marriage. I absolutely resist "prying" into the couple's own intimacy level, since I may become the "intruder" who weakens their bond by exposing it. So in my first session, I tell them both, "I will not be asking intimate questions of you about your relationship with each other. You can count on me to be 'on the side of the angels,' and I want to 'get you to the church on time.'" Pastors sometimes effectively "rape" a marriage by demanding information that belongs exclusively to the couple. They are in direct violation of Jesus' caution: "What therefore God has joined together, let no one put asunder."

I have a clear sense of urgency that we need earlier training for our children on how to spot sexual predators—those promiscuous women and men who carry sexual addiction into legal marriage, only to devastate an otherwise healthy bonding spouse. And, if I knew the young man to whom you refer as well as you seem to know him, I would confront him myself about "truth in marriage," and call him both to repentance and to complete moral and spiritual rehabilitation before his marriage.

4

Grounds for Divorce?

△

After I had opened up Jesus' teaching in Matthew 19 about divorce, Kurt stopped me in the narthex:

"You have no idea what kind of timing God worked in bringing you with that sermon this morning. You have saved my marriage. It would take two hours to tell you."

"Write to me this afternoon," I urged, still hanging on to the grip of the handshake we had begun. He did, and here is the story:

"Last week my wife announced to me that four years ago she had an affair with my college roommate. We had been married for three years and had our first child. I should also tell you that Lila and I were sexually involved for two years before our marriage. So, our honeymoon did not have as special a meaning for us or give us as strong a bond as I think it should have done. It was also necessary for us to ignore God by doing what we both knew to be wrong. I wondered what was wrong with her. I was happy at my work, was gone from twelve to fifteen hours each day, and was baffled to come home and find her in tears. Finally, she arranged to travel two hours away to our university town where we had met. She would stay with one of my suite-mates and his wife. But there she was also going to

61

be near my old roommate who was still unmarried at that time.

"Well, the old roommate was always fond of Lila. They spent time together that week and Bill gave her the feeling of worth that I was neglecting. They followed their feelings all the way to bed. When the week was over, I could tell that something had changed. I never confronted Bill, and Lila always denied that anything had happened. She was sure, she now says, that I would file for divorce.

"Bill has married and now lives nearby. Since the affair, we have not been close. Bill and his wife are not Christians.

"My response hasn't been completely rosy. I've had days when I've felt very insecure. I've cried. Grieved. Other times and days I feel great and very close to Lila. Your sermon on divorce was just what I needed to hear to put a final end to the murmuring in the recesses of my mind that I ought to do just that. But I've never wanted to divorce Lila. I just want to spend the rest of my life with her.

"I had toyed with the idea of an affair myself, before Lila and I talked last week. I had even considered Bill's wife as the target! It would have been revenge of a sort. He puts in long hours at the engineering firm where he is employed and Cheryl is left alone too often.

"I have rearranged my priorities and try to keep Lila and the children in a position just behind God and well ahead of my professional endeavors. My biggest concern now is to put all of this behind me and out of mind—or at least in the right corner of my mind. Right now it colors almost every moment of affection and I look forward to concentrating on her without an occasional question mark popping up in my thoughts."

Everybody Knows the Grounds for Divorce

At Point Loma Nazarene College I raised the question, "What are the grounds for divorce?" It was a trick question I posed for the hundred or so students who showed up in the lecture hall for a look at "Sexual Purity in a Pornographic Age." I wanted to get the students to help me sort out biblical and human development issues defining sexual purity, pornography, fornication, and adultery with its schizophrenic bonding. I waded in on the topic by asking an elementary question, "What are the grounds for divorce?" I immediately had the answer that is universal in the civilized world. No one shouted it, but it formed in unison on a dozen pairs of lips:

"Adultery." I told them that I would accept that for now, but I was going to take it away from them later.

Among religious people in virtually all Judeo-Christian traditions, the "grounds" are thought to come from Scripture. Among the more secular populations, the "grounds" are rooted in simple alienation: "You mess around once, and that's it!" The law of the frontier imposed the death penalty, if the old cowboy legends are reliable. In secular cultures the sinners are usually women. Men seem to have written the rules, and they can get away with almost anything.

Creation and Redemption Agree

The Genesis image of "two becoming one flesh, naked and unashamed," is enhanced by Jesus when he adds, "What God has joined together let no one separate." Between those two peaks lies the valley of broken and damaged relationships between men and women. Divorce was formulated by Moses to regulate the chaos that threatened the community as marriages broke under the weight of the selfishness of hard human hearts. Following the original sin, the consequences were summarized in the words of God to the woman: "Your desire will be for your husband, and he will rule over you" (Gen. 3:16). What had begun as a co-regency and joint-tenancy became a power struggle. The woman's "desire" or eros-based worship of her husband would anchor her and thus perpetuate the intimate bond. Only this mysterious "desire" would sustain her as the man would tend to dominate and rule her, often exploiting and abusing her.

The tragedy of power-based male-female relationships was bridged by Jesus. He insisted twice in the famous Matthew 19 confrontation about divorce that God's design in Genesis 2 is again the vision for the new age. Curiously, many Christians base their marriage and family structure on Genesis 3—the power model in which "he rules over her." Jesus says, "But it was not this way from the beginning. . . ," and again:

> "Haven't you read," he replied, "that at the beginning the Creator 'made them male and female,' and said, 'For this reason a man will leave his father and mother and be united to his wife, and the two will become one flesh'? So they are no longer two, but one. Therefore what God has joined together, let no one separate."
>
> Matthew 19:4–6

In the Mark account of the "divorce" encounter, the consequences of divorce are starkly presented by Jesus: "Anyone who divorces his wife and marries another woman commits adultery against her. And if she divorces her husband and marries another man, she commits adultery" (10:11–12). There is no suggestion that any circumstance can "break" the marriage and justify leaving the marriage and marrying another person without the consequence of "committing adultery." Notice that "adultery," here and everywhere in the words of Jesus, is not cited as the cause for ending a marriage, but is pointed to as the tragic and painful effect that rolls into place when a new bond is established on the ruins of the old bond.

The Gospel of Mark is thought by many people to be the oldest of the Gospels. But it lacks the clear "Jewish" focus of Matthew, evident here both by the omission of the fairly "inside" allusion to the "nakedness" of Deuteronomy 24:1–4, and by the fact that Mark makes it cut both ways: both men and women will be "committing adultery" if they leave one bond and turn to another. Matthew, Luke, and John report only the damaged woman side. Jewish tradition, firmly in the grip of the original sin, regarded women as male property, and male failure was unreported. Both polygamy and prostitution were tolerated within Judaism. Here, as today, the witness of the heathen aspirations for equality between the sexes led the way out of an encrusted, fallen tradition which justified violent use of women. All other Gospel texts assume that divorce or failure in a marriage is targeted on the "disposable wife." Women simply were "property" of males, and had no means whereby to charge a husband with infidelity. It is perhaps ironic that today, as in Jesus' time, there seems often to be more concern for the dignity and value of women in the secular world than in many conservative, fundamental churches.

Luke, in the style of Matthew, levels the entire statement at the husband and states nothing about a divorcing wife: "Anyone who divorces his wife and marries another woman commits adultery, and the man who marries a divorced woman commits adultery" (Luke 16:18). So there is a solid base for concluding that Creation and Redemption agree: God made no plan for multiple partners, double or triple bonding, and divorce or remarriage. Whenever such variations from the Creation-Redemption ideal appear, they are exceptions and call for special grace. Moses did not "command" divorce; he "permitted" it. Both Mark 10 and Matthew 19 agree on the emergency intervention of divorce into the ideal of lifelong marriage. And divorce was permitted specifically to clear the way for remarriage of both partners in the failed marriage. Deuteronomy 24 and Ezra 10 illustrate the use of divorce to return the partners to a legal state of singleness with the expectation that they would remarry.

All of this tragic emergency procedure of divorce was made "law" to deal with the complex problems of a fallen human society. "Because your hearts were hard," Jesus said.

Hardness of Heart . . .

Jesus simply does not suggest any "justifying cause" for leaving a marriage. And "adultery" is the consequence of divorce, not a "grounds" for filing. It is "harlotry" or "fornication" that may dissolve the marital bond while the legal marriage is intact. But there is one "grounds for divorce" which Jesus acknowledges: someone suffers from hardness of heart.

"Why then," they asked, "did Moses command that a man give his wife a certificate of divorce and send her away?"

Jesus replied, "Moses permitted you to divorce your wives because your hearts were hard. But it was not this way from the beginning. I tell you that anyone who divorces his wife, [except for harlotry], and marries another woman commits adultery."

Matthew 19:7–9

Moses did not institute divorce. God made no plan for dissolving a "one-flesh" bond. But "Moses permitted . . . divorce because your hearts were hard." It is easy to see how a couple's hearts might be hardened within a marriage. But the most tender-hearted people are hardened by the divorce action itself.

Billy confided that after Judy left with their three lovely children and filed for divorce, he consulted an attorney. Billy was instructed to write down all of the accusations he could think of and make them look pretty bad, "We're going to go for the whole bag!" his attorney had said.

But Billy told me, "Judy is my best friend, I cannot imagine trying to resurrect small quarrels and slinging mud at her character to try to get the kids. She would never come back to me if I did that."

Regrettably, hardness of heart may lead to divorce, whether the hardness is an intentional rebellion, as in the case of Pharaoh in Egypt hardening his heart against God, or as in the case of an embattled marriage where the callouses of months or years of abuse erode the affection. Creation and redemption agree: nothing need destroy a marriage, but sometimes a marriage has to be abandoned so that the people can get on with reconstructing life. In such a case, the whole universe groans and any caring community learns to "weep with those who weep."

Except for . . .

The phrase, "except for harlotry/fornication" does not appear in the Mark 10:1–12 version, but does show up both in Matthew 5:32 and 19:9. Even so, it is not a justifying condition, but a description of a certain kind of default that may prevent the marital bond from setting up. Or once set up, its effects may have dissolved the "one-flesh" attachment, clearing the way for a future relationship unencumbered by the schizophrenia of a double-bonded, adulterated marriage. *Porneia*—the fornication trap—based as it is on mere instrumental "use" of persons for sexual pleasure, may bring together either sexually or in legal marriage two persons "unequally yoked." The fornicating spouse, in the text of a current country and western lyric, came "only for fun." So the one who came "for love" finds no mutually formed bond, and the dream of "one flesh, naked, unashamed, forever" is dashed.

Matthew's "Jewish audience" would have been aware of the Deuteronomy text which described terms under which divorce was permitted. And it may be that the "harlotry/fornication" phrase is a direct "quote" by Jesus from its single "condition." Look at the passage:

If a man marries a woman who becomes displeasing to him [because he finds something indecent about her], and he writes her a certificate of divorce, gives it to her and sends her from his house, and if after she leaves his house she becomes the wife of another man, and her second husband dislikes her and writes her a certificate of divorce, gives it to her and sends her from his house, or if he dies, then her first husband, who divorced her, is not allowed to marry her again after she has been defiled. That would be destestable in the eyes of the Lord. Do not bring sin upon the land the Lord your God is giving you as an inheritance.

Deuteronomy 24:1–4

If you compare the bracketed phrases in Matthew 19, above, with the bracketed clause here in Deuteronomy 24, we may have further light on the one condition which dissolves the Creation glue in the "one-flesh" bond. The "indecency" in Deuteronomy is literally "naked thing."[1] Promiscuity, or the inability to "keep your clothes on," or "your trousers up" may easily link the "harlotry/fornication" of Matthew 5 and 19 with the one condition permitted for dissolving a marriage.

But we must satisfy ourselves that "fornication/harlotry" is different from "adultery," and must explore how adultery is a consequence of divorce. We may also want to find what redeeming hope there is for curing adultery and what strategies might help in curing "indecency/nakedness" and "harlotry/fornication."

Effects of Addiction on a Marriage

The King James Version translated harlotry as "fornication." Modern translations take extreme liberties when they translate the term as "marital unfaithfulness," since it is consistently used elsewhere to denote instrumental sexual addiction. The root word, *porneia,* is the stem from which we get pornography. It is translated "harlot," "whore," "prostitute," and "whoremonger."

A "harlotry person" is obviously a promiscuous, sexually addicted person. Even marriage is sometimes used as an "instrumental object."

"I wanted to be married more than anything else," a woman once told Robbie and me. For two hours she grieved over the canceled marriage, the wasted money for wedding and attendant gowns, lost status, and the embarrassment of having a diamond but no groom. Never in that time did she show any grief over the loss of a friend or lover. He was never named with any tears—only the grief of instrumental loss. Among the fast lane crowd, there sometimes comes a sense that "it is time to marry." But one's sexual appetite, once addicted to pleasure for the sake of pleasure alone, does not settle easily into a bonded marriage.

Porneia—differs from *moicheia,* which is translated "adultery" in English—consistently points to sexual activities which are mere functional and instrumental uses of sex for self-centered pleasure. Other people may be used, but the ultimate purpose is not to bring them pleasure or to be joined in "one flesh, naked and unashamed, until death do us part." Prostitution is a clear example of *porneia.* But so, also, are incest, and all pornographic uses of film, print media, and imagination: looking to lust after another's body for the pleasure it would bring the self.

When I ask what "fornication" is, I consistently get the instant, if muffled response: "unmarried lovers." Yet nowhere in Holy Scripture is it used to describe sexual intimacy between lovers who are exclusively committed to each other. We have blurred our own understanding of the Bible's teaching on human sexuality by bringing narrow and incorrect stereotypes to words we try not to think about between readings.

"Fornication" is a tragedy because it describes the effects of sexual addiction. Such people lose their capacity for sexual bonding with one exclusive partner, and quickly regard persons as objects to be used. Unmarried lovers run a high risk, of course, since they may not be able to protect their love affair and the fragile bond that is forming may be ripped apart as they are discovered or as their circumstances take them away from each other. In such cases, the sexual appetite is vulnerable to quick-developing sexual exchanges with near strangers, and "fornication" may then set in as a long-term damage to the core of personality. Both *porneia* and *moicheia*—fornication and adultery—are tragedies. But they are very different ones, so St. Paul lists both in the deadly series in 1 Corinthians:

Do you not know that the wicked will not inherit the kingdom of God? Do not be deceived: Neither *fornicators* nor idolaters nor *adulterers* nor male prostitutes nor homosexual offenders nor thieves nor the greedy nor drunkards nor slanderers nor swindlers will inherit the kingdom of God. And that is what some of you were. But you were washed, you were sanctified, you were justified in the name of the Lord Jesus Christ and by the Spirit of our God.

1 Corinthians 6:9–11

If "fornication" were simply "adultery" between unmarried lovers, Paul would hardly have needed to list them separately. For anyone who wishes to sort out the fornication passages, they consistently speak of promiscuous, non-bonding, predator use of other people for sexual gratification. Look again at chapter 2 for sorting through the distinction between fornication and adultery.

And on the brightest note possible, notice here that Paul does not suggest that "some of you used to be fornicators, adulterers, male prostitutes, and homosexual offenders, but God called you to celibacy and holiness." Just the opposite must be true: Having failed in intimate relationships, they have now been redeemed in their continuing, remarried, or otherwise sanctified life patterns, and there is no suggestion that they must pay for their sins by living without a Creation "one-flesh" bond within God's male-female image.

The Matthew phrase, however, suggests there may be something about fornication/harlotry which profoundly flaws a marital bond. The effects of that flaw may prevent the marital bond from setting up, such that one who divorces does not experience "double bonding" or "adultery" upon remarrying.

But in no case does a marriage need to break, even if a sexual predator or *porneia* person is involved. St. Paul cautions that a healthy person may become bonded to a fornicator: "Do you not know that he who unites himself with a prostitute is one with her in body?" (1 Cor. 6:16). Instead, if we use the model of Hosea in pursuit of his errant wife Gomer, the spouse may choose to pursue the wayward one to bring the beloved back to sexual fidelity and wholeness. God never abandoned Israel when she "played the harlot." There is simply no breakdown in sexual behavior which automatically calls for the end of a relationship or a marriage.

And here is precisely where adultery and fornication sometimes overlap. A promiscuous person may pursue and even marry a healthy bonding person. Their intimacy will result, in the very same experiences, in "fornication" or instrumental use by the promiscuous person, and in "adultery" or affectional bonding for the healthy, bonding person. The classical way of showing the relationship between *porneia* and *moicheia* has been to say that fornication was an all-encompassing term in Scripture, of which adultery was a smaller sub-section:

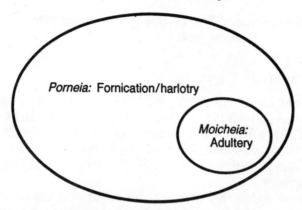

But any massive reading of Old Testament and New Testament uses of fornication/prostitution/harlotry compared to "adultery" shows them to be distinctly different from each other. Both are ultimately destructive. But a progression tends to occur by which a person's innocence is either preserved lifelong by fidelity and permanent bonding, or it gets off the track into "bonding" which turns out to be in series, leading to promiscuity and the lack of ability to bond in a healthy way. So we might diagram the two tragic conceptualizations more accurately in this way:

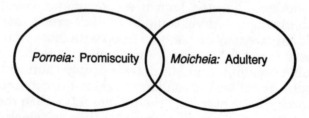

So here is a Scripture picture of John Schneider's plaintive country and western lyric. He describes having stepped out on his wife who is an angel. But the sweet temptation turned sour and tragic when his secret extramarital lover "took for fun" what he "took for love." The adultery constituted a "short walk from heaven to hell"! Curiously, I find in my occasional car-radio listening to country and western lyrics that they fall nicely into the three categories I unfolded in chapter 3: *porneia,* the virginal dream, adultery.

Try categorizing a few of the lyrics when you next find them in the air about you.

Where Adultery Comes In

The so-called "exception phrase" in Matthew 5 and 19 simply seems to indicate that sometimes there is no bond established to haunt the remarriage of a divorcing spouse. But for those who leave a sexual bond, the "double bonding" or "adultery" will stalk the life of both, should they end the marriage.

But look again, try moving the exception clause nearer to the issue it addresses: "I tell you that anyone who divorces his wife and marries another woman commits adultery [except a person who divorces because of harlotry]."

This rearrangement of the phrase puts the tragedy of adultery in focus. What is clear here, confronting both the churchly and the pagan tradition, is this: adultery is not a justifying cause for divorce, regardless of how you read the rhetoric of the Matthew passages. Adultery is the painful ghost that goes into the next marriage. Fornication/harlotry/whoremongering might seem to justify a divorce, but in no case does adultery do so. What would happen if Christians suddenly became known as the unique community of faith in which nothing could in itself destroy a marriage?

Suddenly we may be ready to weep with those who weep. Adultery is not a "grounds" for divorce. It is the tragedy of double bonding. And Matthew is simply cautioning that if a couple is not very careful in weighing the consequences of divorcing they may hurt themselves more than they can imagine: they will set off a chain reaction in which "adultery" is the tragic aftershock to divorce. And here we strike a fundamental key to our misunderstanding of adultery.

What Double Bonding Does to a Marriage

When we discuss the death penalty versus life imprisonment for "first-degree murder" we are not focusing on the legal aspect of the jurisprudence system. We are discussing the tragic loss of a human life at the hand of another human who deliberately and maliciously snuffed out the most precious possession in all the world: life itself.

Yet, most of the conversations you have heard about "adultery" have focused on the legal and moral implications surrounding somebody's playing around. What we miss, in all of this, is the appropriate grief we might express when we name the tragic word: a grand and peaceable bond between two persons has been assaulted and perhaps dealt a mortal blow. And what is worse, nothing in all of time can erase the memory of the alien bond which stole away a lover. Next time you hear the word adultery, try to compare your emotional response to that you might have felt if the word, instead, had been "murder." "Adultery" tends to be treated as a "moral" word, but "murder" still shocks us with feelings of raw tragedy. But both murder and adultery denote stark and naked tragedy.

"I feel like a leper in my church. 'Divorced' is a scarlet letter, for whatever reason the marriage has been lost," one woman told me.

"And I can survive the censure from my church. It is the haunting ghost of our flawless marriage of seven years that haunts me now, ten years after the divorce and my husband's remarriage. We had everything going for us that any couple could have wanted. And it is gone, now, forever. The children and I will never be quite the same as we might have been."

The "ghost" which haunts life after divorce is the echo of a lost but once treasured bond. If a spouse is lost through death, the memory is strong, but it tends to be positive and affirming. But a bond broken by a living and breathing former lover tends to leave the pain and scars of "what might have been made of a love that began with greatness," to use the description of one grieving man. This lingering bond sets the stage for the tragedy which comes uninvited into remarriage while the grieving is in progress. I call adultery, therefore, "double bonding." At its best, it constitutes a "ghost" of intimacy past; at its worse it is schizophrenic bonding—in which ambivalence stalks the heart and while loving one, the fantasy is victim of the other.

The Creation picture is of one woman and one man

magnetically attached to each other: one flesh. This primal image seems also to be written deeply into the universal human dream. But the capacity to become sexually attracted and bonded to additional partners is also a universal liability.

The famous Masters and Johnson team of sex therapists in Saint Louis reported on "swinging couples" in their popular book, *The Pleasure Bond.* If the idea of "sleeping around" in an "open marriage" seems exotic, their findings were shockingly straight. One year after the interviews with four couples and one "trio" the research team found none of the participants still "swinging." All but one of the couples, "Joan and Kyle Sanders," emerged from their sexual swinging experiences "seeking an improved sense of personal security." Only the Sanders couple "seemed to have a relationship in which each partner felt safe with the other."[2]

While the Masters and Johnson sample was inadequate as a major research base, they cite the periodic interviews with the couples in their search for "what fidelity means in a marriage." One "swinging couple" divorced between interview dates, but the others had quit simply because they needed more time together. All of this is reported by the most secular of sex therapy teams. But after pioneering with efforts to treat sexual problems with the use of "surrogate" partners, they concluded that sexual dysfunction must necessarily be treated within the caring relationship of a fully committed partner if effects are to persist in the long term. These sex researchers sound a vigorous caution to those clergy who take a soft attitude toward sexual fidelity. They cite both Protestant and Catholic authors who take a light view of sexual infidelity, then extend a three-page critical analysis typified by these words:

> It is one thing to repudiate the idea that every instance of extramarital sex is an anathema to God; it is something else to advance the idea that in certain cases extramarital sex is a way of being faithful to God. Such a suggestion, coming from authorities who are concerned with the ethics of sex, is doubly dangerous. Not only does it lend itself to the most seductive

of rationalizations but it undermines the value of sexual commitment by subordinating the exclusive physical bond between
husband and wife to the apparent needs of a third person.[3]

"Double bonding" which sets the stage for adultery and
its unique stress on a marriage typically occurs when extended common experience brings the aliens together—
one or both of whom are previously, exclusively bonded
to a lover or a spouse. I must stress that genital intimacy
is not necessary to establish the original bond or a second
alien bond. With persons who have no previous genital experience, the tragic tearing of the "double bond" dilemma
is likely as traumatic as is the case of genital contact and
physical adultery. Jesus was right to say that "whoever looks
and lusts is guilty of adultery in the heart." It is the establish-
ing of the bonding sequence to any of the highest four
stages of pair bonding which sets off the riptides of emotional distress when bonds are competing for loyalty.[4]
One of the frequent signs of the development of the alien
bond is a declining interest in sexual intimacy in the marriage. The intrinsic "monogamous" moral sense often causes
the wandering spouse to shut down intimacy in the marriage even before it is established in adultery. But such a
"slow down" is by no means proof of an alien threat, and,
in fact, some unfaithful spouses actually increase the amo-
rous behavior with the spouse in what they later describe
as "vicarious rehearsal" of intimacy with the new lover.
These two patterns, opposite to each other, seem to follow
the basic patterning I have described elsewhere as "monogamous, exclusive pair-bonding" people in contrast to "tournament species" people, usually males.[5]
In a documentary on the covert polygamous marriages
of a Mormon sect in the United States, a television news
special showed film footage of interviews with both the husbands and the multiple wives. Repeatedly the women reported having difficulty adapting to the idea of "sharing"
the husband as he announced his intentions to take a new
wife. While perhaps a half-dozen men were interviewed
on camera, none of them expressed similar feelings of ambivalence at acquiring multiple bonds. It would be easy to

conclude that males are not as faithful in their bonding as are women. But to test the hypothesis, one would have to study both men and women in a reverse culture where a woman acquired a harem of men.

There is enough "egocentrism" in most of us, I suspect, for us to "lord it over" the other sex if we could justify the exploitation on any shred of legal or religious foundation. We would likely pursue self-gratification physically, financially, or socially in terms of status and power, if we were fairly sure we could justify it. Only God's redeeming grace can change that central tendency to serve the self. Polygyny of any sort must put stresses on the human need for lifelong, exclusive, one-flesh bonding which pushes the personality structure to the wall.

Dan, I had thought, was promiscuous. There had been three "affairs" across ten years or so. When I inquired about venereal disease he might have brought home, he gave me a sidelong look that communicated his deep hurt. He was an adulterer, he was letting me know, but he was not "sleeping around." Promiscuous people, it turns out, experience very little pain or guilt in losing partners. They were, after all, not interested in "persons" but in sex—and any convenient, attractive partner would do. Dan was distinctly not promiscuous or sexually addicted. He was double-bonded. At that final session when he phoned and drove to my office at considerable inconvenience to himself, I was to see the tragic depth of his double attachment:

"Try writing a final letter to June," I suggested. "Tell her exactly what you feel for her and what losing her is going to cost you."

Dan sat there as in shock. He had not at that time let his emotion out with me through tears, though they would flow profoundly before the session ended. When I saw the seriousness with which he was contemplating a final break with June, the other woman, I added:

"If you cannot break with June and return to Mary and the children, then try a different letter. Write one to Mary and to the children. Explain to them what they mean to you and how hard it is to break away from them—what it is going to cost you and them for you to go with June."

How a Marriage Dies

Experts on a "theology of divorce" not only tend to misunderstand the distinction between fornication and adultery; they also tend to miss the one tragic "cause" Jesus cites for divorce: "Jesus replied, Moses permitted you to divorce your wives because your hearts were hard. But it was not this way from the beginning . . .'" (Matt. 19:8).

"Hardness of heart" becomes, therefore, in some tragic sense, the "only biblical grounds for divorce." You can read the phrase "hardening of the heart" through any chain-reference or topical study Bible. It is clear that the scarring of affection, whether deliberate or simply "cumulative," brings on a dullness of attention to or attraction toward a once-respected, magnetic Other. More often than not the "hardness of heart" is a callous tissue which deadens the responsiveness of a person toward God. "Pharaoh hardened his heart" toward God, for example. And here is a critical feature: most often, the hardening occurs either by a decision or with the consent of the will. Thus, anyone might choose—perhaps grounded in *agape* love—to love unconditionally, even to confront in order to stop the erosion of love.

No intimate relationship collapses simply under its own weight. But any marriage may collapse, or love die in any relationship if attention and affection cease to be a priority. And should the priority slip in the wake of a harried vocational or pleasure pursuit, we move into some categories which signal serious trouble. When these are visible in a relationship, the probability of "hardening of the heart" is greatly increased.

It is "narcissism," the love of self, that drives all of the patterns which set up hardness of heart—from sexual addiction to the lust for power and dominion and control in a marriage. Let me list and illustrate some of those patterns I have observed in marriages which ended—mostly because neither of the partners was willing or able to end the pattern. And the good news is that either partner is able to "change" the relationship by changing their role in the destructive transactions:

1. *Power.*—If males plummet out of the marriage altar's "co-regency and joint-tenancy" right down to the demonic "he shall rule over her," females tend to follow quickly in deadly pursuit with: "I'll show him a thing or two." The central tendency, perhaps because of what happened so long ago in Eden, is for every marriage to slip into a vertical power struggle. What males can boast in brawn is easily matched by an intuitive and clever brain. This adversary positioning in a marriage tends to shut down the affectional system that is young and fragile. Conflict over money, sex, children, schedules, vocation, social patterns, and even matters of faith are only a few of the issues that a vertical, adversary positioned marriage will confront. And with the battle positions well assaulted, the marital pair bond is in for some severe testing.

2. *Fraud.*—Occasionally the wedding day ends the "search for intimacy." Some lovers pursue a partner primarily for security. Then, once a spouse is in hand, they turn their attention to more materialistic, vocational matters. There is enough of this cooling down of intimacy to evoke a cultural outcry against it. One "living together" couple told me, "We have a better relationship than do any of our friends who are married. They were really considerate of each other until they were married, then they quit and started fighting. We don't want to get into that." St. Paul cautions against letting the fires of intimate love go out:

> The husband should fulfill his marital duty to his wife, and likewise the wife to her husband. The wife's body does not belong to her alone but also to her husband. In the same way, the husband's body does not belong to him alone but also to his wife. Do not deprive each other except by mutual consent and for a time, so that you may devote yourselves to prayer. Then come together again so that Satan will not tempt you because of your lack of self-control.
>
> 1 Corinthians 7:3–5

Intimacy is both the launching ramp for a lifelong exclusive bond and also the daily maintenance of the "one-flesh/one-person" relationship.

3. *Abuse.*—Physical assault or verbal assault do not immediately cancel the affectional bond. In fact abused children tend at a very high rate to marry abusive spouses, perhaps because they have confused the physical contact through abuse with the "skin hunger" for tender loving. But a more subtle abuse occurs when, over a period of months and years, one of the partners sends signals to the other about marks of inferior performance or appearance or abilities. Such an innocent factor as personality structure may weasel itself into a husband-wife relationship and set off a fatal blow to a marriage. For example, if a husband is an "extraverted, intuitive, thinking, judging type" on the Myers-Briggs personality type indicator and the wife is an "intraverted, sensing, feeling, judging type,"[6] several land mines may explode over time: (1) She will likely spend some years at home bearing children. This complicates her intraverted world which, while it thrives on quiet and privacy, can leave her feeling isolated. She may lack the initiative to force her way into the outer world with its healthy perspective.

(2) If he is creative and mobile, he may bounce into the house occasionally to check, but he lacks the "feeling" sensitivity which has been overruled by his "thinking" gifts, and he is unlikely to remember to express affection, only looking after tangible needs and running along to his next important meeting.

(3) If she sees a way to improve their circumstances, she will volunteer it—for a few months or years at the most—and he will criticize it intellectually; though he may modify it and act on it later, it will then seem to her to be really "his" idea, since he criticized her apparently naive suggestion. This sort of subtle psychological abuse is fed by both sides: she operates out of her "feeling" and so lapses into self-condemnation until she is considering suicide; he operates out of his "thinking" and has her "figured out." She needs counseling. She has a problem. And the once powerful bond that would have fought off wild Indians is now reduced to disintegrating powder at their feet.

4. *Competition.*—"I married you to stay at home and be here when I come home. I want you to resign from the

Racquet Club and quit coaching the church women's softball team. And I simply will not have you working on a master's degree, at least not now." Put the scenario together any way you like it. In the more traditional scene, it is the man who is threatened by a woman who strives for competency, vocation, and education. But these days I am sometimes hearing it from women who insist on pushing it to the top and demanding that their husbands get a "mobile" job to follow the wife's career. While these look like "power moves" and bear similarities to the struggles outlined in the "power" section, there is a difference: Here there is often a battle to be "first," to "outdo" the spouse. When they were in college they "fought to the death" over ping-pong or a "trivia" game. They threw the pieces of a Monopoly set at each other if the breaks went the wrong way. This is the "winning at any cost" instinct. The marital bond is threatened by competition. It will thrive on "cooperation." When "two become one" there may be two dreams or two life visions, but there are now the combined resources of the "one-flesh" union to discover how to achieve all of the dreams and to surrender self-interest to "couple" and "family" interests.

5. *Default.*—But it is the "rat race" that kills more marriages than any other predator. Call it "neglect," or "sloth," if you like. The honeymoon was wonderful, even if it did run up the fourth major debt—the first being a diamond, the second the wedding, and the third a car. Now they settle in to the 7-to-7 routine of school or work or both. Where they once looked into each other's eyes and read the inner needs, loves, and hurts, they now stare into the TV or the newspaper, or drift through the early morning fog, grabbing coffee from a vending machine on the way to the first shift or class. It is this creeping, calloused behavior that frightens young lovers, some of whom commit suicide lest they should live to see their idyllic love turn into a plastic carton called an "apartment" and into plastic gestures called "making love" when there is so little evidence that real caring is present at all.

I have overdrawn the scenario, of course, but if the twelve steps of the pair bond are not renewed on an almost daily basis, the bond will erode, communication and trust will go out of a marriage. In the "olden days" couples would continue to go through the motions of marriage and family and live as mannequins in the house. But with extended life spans and higher expectations in a marriage, it is essential that we learn the first lessons in bonding and develop lifelong variations on their rich themes.[7]

If You Have Been Divorced

"Vulnerable." That is perhaps the continuing emotional state of the divorced. "Hurt," "crushed," "numb" are other words I hear.

You are likely to conclude that you have failed in the one important vocation in life: being a man, a husband, and a father; or being a woman, a wife, and a mother. Whenever we look at the grand possibilities in human intimacy and the splendor of the ideal of exclusive, monogamous, "one flesh, naked and unashamed" marriage it is tempting to write off the whole thing as (a) an impossible dream, or (b) possible for a few, but out of my reach.

And here we confront an amazing paradox. The perfect vision of perfect love in human relationships is a dream worth pursuing. Whether most of us achieve it at the level we want is less important than that it hang out there as God's target toward which we aspire. So, I spend most of my time encouraging people to polish the lenses and mirrors in their telescopes so as to bring the grand planet of perfect marriage closer.

But at the same time, I am equally eager to scramble to my knees to help you pick up the shattered pieces of your dream and to present them to the great Healer. My favorite two-line theology says simply:

> *God, who has created all things good,*
> *Can make all things new, through Jesus!*

So, I conclude that (a) no marriage is beyond repair, through God's grace, and (b) no life is so tragically scarred, but that it can be healed and made new again by the grace of God's Son Jesus. Chapters 5 and 6 are entirely devoted to the two patterns for reconstruction where fornication/promiscuity or adultery may have dealt a mortal blow to the "heart" of a marriage. Until then, I want to unfold some first tips for getting healing under way if you suffer from divorce. You will find the Gospel details which undergird the divorcing person in chapters 5 and 6, but know that it is the *actions* of Jesus of Nazareth from which I also take my cues. Only when they undergird his *words* about marital failure and divorce do we have a fully orbed teaching from Jesus.[8] Here are some tips for now, if you have lost a marriage or an important relationship for any reason:

Time is the great resource of those who lose their marriages and with that, very often, their dreams. I will discuss, in chapter 6, some ways to "come back" when divorce strikes. During any grief or shock it is important that no major decisions are made. Decisions about where to live, and whether to remarry should be delayed until the shock waves and the first grief are past.

"I will never marry again," a young sailor told me more than thirty years ago when I was his family's pastor.

"I understand your feelings, I think. But when God brings healing to your broken heart, there will be plenty of time to see whether you are able to love a good and gracious woman."

Not long ago our phone rang. It was the two adult children of that young sailor. They phoned from Dallas in hopes that the pastor who married their Daddy and Mother could be present for the twenty-fifth anniversary. We were unable, but we phoned right into the gala celebration that honored the solid and faithful marriage of a man whose dream was shattered and his innocence eroded by a divorce that came while he was on the high seas in military service.

Besides time, divorced people need a *network* of folks around them who are unconditionally committed to their survival and their health. Sometimes these are the people who help hold to the time delay for two to four years, minimum, to bring recovery, healing, and the perspective that anyone needs to make decisions about another relationship.[9]

Ultimately, every person needs to mount a *serious pursuit of God's righteousness, justice, mercy, and love.* There is no surer path than to surrender all of life to Jesus and to let him breathe new life into old dreams. But they will be new dreams appropriate to the new circumstance and consistent with the character of Jesus.

Divorce and Remarriage: Some Biblical Perspectives

Let me summarize where all of this exploration leaves us on divorce. Here are the main lines, which are really very simple. They hold to a most elegant view of one-flesh, exclusive, lifelong bonding, and at the same time encircle the broken and grieving victims of lost relationships and marriages:[10]

1. Lifelong, exclusive, one-flesh, monogamous, male-female intimacy is God's Creation design for humans. Any variation from that design places the created human under stress and pain as reminders that we were made for the peaceable exclusive relationship.

2. When the marital bond is carefully and patiently formed, it is virtually indestructible. God, Jesus, Moses, and Paul all agree that there is no self-justifying "grounds for divorce," not even promiscuity or adultery. Anyone who suggests to another person that they have "grounds for divorce" is likely revealing that they themselves suffer from "hardness of heart" and do not understand that love is stronger than death.

3. When a divorce occurs, it is a signal that the marital bond has suffered a mortal blow. Most often, the death of the bond is triggered by a hard-hearted, intentional act of violence against the marriage by one of the partners. Hardening of the affection, either deliberately or slowly over time, turns marital partners into an inevitable adversary relationship sometimes making divorce necessary.

4. God never designed divorce, but through the community of Israel God regulated it to minimize the tragic effects of abandoned and broken bonds. The regulation was in the form of divorce to allow people to escape a dead marriage and to start over again.

5. Sexual addiction—such as the indecency of harlotry and/or promiscuity—can destroy the one-flesh bond by dis-

solving its Creation mystery glue, leading to the death of a bond.

6. Tender-hearted people always use their own ingenuity and the resources of their support network to find a way to redeem a marriage, regardless of what may have troubled it.

7. Nevertheless, divorce is sometimes inevitable, since either of the two persons have individual and ultimate power to end a marriage.

8. If a divorce occurs, tender-hearted people will "buy time" and will actively seek outside, seasoned, objective counsel to gain perspective and facilitate healing, while making decisions about appropriate steps to take regarding the primary bond and any future needs for affection and intimacy. During this time they will work for restoration of the original bond.

9. However, divorce for any reason is not the end of the world. Jesus can heal and restore any of us who has been deeply scarred by the loss of a relationship or a marriage, including the sexually addicted as well as the most frozen-up and emotionally damaged person.

10. So long as the spouse remains single, there is hope for re-uniting the tender-hearted, open, and faith-loving people. To be tender-hearted is to own the truth, to repent of the destruction and tragedy of the loss of the marriage, and to set about to make restitution to oneself and to the spouse and others who have been damaged by the failing marriage.

11. Marriage is a "corporate" experience, and its loss is a corporate loss; so repentance is appropriate: there are no "innocent" persons who escape undamaged by the tragedy of loss. Mutual grief and ownership of the tragedy are the core issues for repentance and they are necessary for reconciliation.

12. Under any circumstance, when perspective returns, when the restitution and terminal work is done, the way is open for remarriage. There is no "punishment by celibacy" required for persons whose marriage is lost, hopelessly dead after long, careful time in mature grief and reconstruction. Celibacy is for the voluntary pre-marital or

post-marital surrender of sexual intimacy for the sake of devoting full energy to the vocation of service to God.

13. The only biblical prohibition against remarriage is for remarrying an "indecent" spouse after one has been married to another, the promiscuity pattern revisited. Sensitive, believing Christians are forbidden even to separate from one another, lest the needs for intimacy drive them to other sinning. They are to remain together so as to keep the door open for restitution, forgiveness, and reconciliation. There is no suggestion that divorced Christians may never remarry. Look at the text in any translation. Here is the New International Version: "To the married I give this command (not I, but the Lord): A wife must not separate from her husband. But if she does, she must remain unmarried or else be reconciled to her husband. And a husband must not divorce his wife" (1 Corinthians 7:10–11).

A Tender-Hearted People

If a marriage can survive literally anything so long as there is a tenderness toward each other, a willingness to own responsibility for the relationship, and a perception that the marriage belongs to the two persons together, then the "tender heart" becomes the priority. Here are some characteristics I have seen in sensitive, mature people:

1. When being "put down" by a spouse's rage, the tender heart still treasures the person and rises up to minister to the other: "You must be very angry and tired. Let me take some of the pressure off of you." Or, "I love you very much, and God knows I don't want to make life difficult for you. Help me find a way not to be a source of irritation for you." Tender-hearted people are not neurotics who pout and take the blame for everything. But they always begin by assuming, "I could do something about this troubled relationship, and I will work from 'my side of the table,' since that is the one I can manage without infringing on my spouse."

2. Tender-hearted people are indestructible, because they are honest, committed to purity and integrity in all relationships. No matter what happens, they are characterized

by hope and patience and continual positive regard toward all other people.

3. When they hear of some tragic "indecency," their first impulse is to burst into tears at the loss of innocence and fidelity in others' marriages. They weep instead of calling on the God-squad to strike somebody dead.

4. They are always people of open arms, willingly welcoming and protecting the failing and the wounded, even the fornicators and adulterers, and they long for the day that healing can come to all of the people affected by a failing marriage. They are quick to reach out, but are slow to express judgment, wrath, or to censure or exclude.

It is, after all, the meek who survive to inherit the earth—those who either by choice or by circumstance have been subjected to severe discipline. And all who have suffered, for whatever reason, tend to be made mellow if their hearts are tender. "Those who take the sword shall perish by the sword," Jesus once said. And Edwin Markham extended it to other spheres:

> The robber is robbed by his riches.
> The tyrant is dragged by his chains.
> The schemer is snared by his cunning.
> The slayer lies dead by the slain.

The alternative, also grounded in Scripture, is "a soft answer turns away wrath."

In this chapter I have wanted to reconstruct the tragic grounds for divorce and to dissolve the easy solution of "adultery" which we have tended to use—and by which we have, all of us, if only by our nodding silence—to "put asunder what God had joined together." I have wanted you to look over my shoulder to examine the very different effects promiscuity/fornication have on a marriage compared to the effects of adultery. And I have wanted you to look at the best words of healing and hope I know for people who, for whatever reason, find themselves divorcing or divorced. I hope you come away from all of this with a truly "tender heart" both for yourself and for all around you. Perhaps we could add some lines of our own to those graphic and tragic ones of Edwin Markham:

Violence can be tamed with gentleness.
Accusations wane with "tell me more."
Blame fades when both help pick up the pieces.
And infidelity dies when love lives.

QUESTIONS PEOPLE ASK

*Q: From your list of words for fornication—harlotry, har-
lot, prostitute, whore, whoremonger—it sounds as if there
are more words for sexually addicted women than for similarly deformed men. How do you account for that?*
A: You are exactly right. Kevin Leman in his *Sex Begins
in the Kitchen* notes in a humorous-tragic reminder that
there are many more words for female genitals and breasts
than for male genitals. Especially at the street and closet
level these terms are almost completely bent toward violence, crudity, and obscenity. And it is likely not by accident
that we have more colorful language for describing evil
women than we have for describing evil men. The reason
for this unequal treatment is clearly rooted in male control
of the typical social order. It is also, no doubt, the reason
behind all of the divorce regulations written to permit men
to get rid of unsatisfactory wives by divorce. In "tournament
species" cultures,[11] the promiscuous males who dominate
harems of women tend to impose death penalties and humil-
iations of all sorts on women who fail to please them. But
the ideal of joint-tenant, co-regency, monogamous marriage
has always been present in the Judeo-Christian vision.

The woman "as property" or as "the womb for unborn
children in a male's loins" has further tilted the language
of marriage and divorce. In ancient times, it was assumed
that males carried the offspring in the semen and that the
woman provided only a womb in which the child grew
until birth. This misunderstanding of conception and the
encoding of both parents' genes into the new person led
to a purely "instrumental" view of women: they were easily
regarded as property. If a woman could not make babies
fast enough or was infertile altogether, then concubines
and multiple wives could solve the problem for the male
who wished to build his labor force and guarantee his tribal
survival.

Today's divorce practices are almost the reverse of those of Jesus' and Moses' days. Then, men got rid of women for the most trivial of reasons, retained possession of all property, and kept the children as their own. Today, women are more likely to keep the residence, negotiate for favorable financial distribution of resources and alimony or child support, and tend to keep the children and take them into a new marriage. The contrast is an important one to keep in mind when reading biblical material on divorce, if only to remind us that divorce is consistently a ripping and tearing event, leaving tragedy in its wake. We can rejoice that women are no longer regarded as mere property or chattel, and that the courts of most Western countries protect them far better than they were protected in Moses' and Jesus' time.

5

Is There Life after Promiscuity?

△

I met Jane when she was thirty-three. She was engaged to be married—and very excited about it. Her fiancé was one of my students, and I had heard of Jane long before I met her. Her reputation for easy sex had been in the community for most of ten years—long before Bob had met her. I had, from a considerable distance, learned that it was Jane who had been the occasion of first one, then another, male seminary student leaving school and his vocation. During those years I did not even know Jane on sight. But now I was to meet her.

Jane's story was grounded in family incest from age twelve when her oldest brother, a senior in high school, forced her into more than a year of fear-dominated sex. When he left home, her second brother, then sixteen, took up where the older brother left off. Then a third brother used her in the same way, all without detection by the parents.

When Jane began dating, it was with her brothers' friends, and sex was the immediate dating game. At sixteen she quietly had her first of several abortions, and by the time I met her she had slept with more than fifty different men over a period of twenty-one years. And now she was in love with Bob, and Bob with her. Would I do the premarital counseling?

Fornication and Sexual Addiction

"Fornication" is one of those antiquated "moralistic" words, but it is the base from which we also get "pornography."[1] And the meaning of fornication, as we saw in chapter 3, simply means "sexual pleasure for its own sake." So a "pornicating" person is not entering into a relationship, but is simply going through the motions of intimacy for other reasons: pleasure, getting the much-needed stroking and touching, earning a living as in the case of the prostitute of either sex, or carrying out a strategy of abuse on the other sex.

"Sexual addiction" today denotes those people who move repeatedly through cycles of compulsive sexual behavior, inevitably putting themselves and other people at serious risk. They consistently make "instrumental use" of people, film, and print material in chronic, sometimes nearly perpetual fantasy. Sex Addicts Anonymous (S.A.A.) is a fellowship of men and women who share their experience, strength, and hope with each other so that they may solve their common problem and help others recover from their sexual addictions. The only requirement for membership is a desire to stop compulsive sexual behavior. They affirm three things: (1) That they are sexually addicted and cannot manage their own lives. (2) That probably no human power can relieve their addictive behavior. And (3) that God can and will relieve them if God is sought. The questionnaire for self-diagnosis is in the appendix: Sexual Addiction: An Inventory from S.A.A., on pp. 155–158.[2]

There are several paths that tend to lead into sexual addiction. Let me describe some I have heard about as the victims reconstructed their histories. Some of the paths are more often followed by males and others by females, though any path may lead a person into the agony of sexual addiction. And, curiously, there may be another factor altogether which sexual addiction has in common across the pathways. Uniformly, the fornicator suffers from extremely low self-esteem. It may be, of course, that the pathological low self-esteem is a result of promiscuity and not a cause at all. On the other hand, none of the pathways I will describe is an inevitable road to sexual addiction. I observe people who have had "close encounters" and have quickly turned away from sexual addiction. These tend to have in common a high degree of "other-centered" empathy or care. I mention these two general characteristics because I want to stress that "nothing that happens to you has an inevitable destiny locked in." There are too many variables for such airtight prediction. But these are, nonetheless, "patterns" I have observed.

Incest. —Jane's case of repeated "sibling incest" is typical of effects on both boys and girls who are introduced to sexual intimacy by a respected or feared relative. Exploration between peer relatives almost never leaves the scar of sexual addiction. Indeed, some form of "playing doctor" in the innocence of childhood has been found by research at the University of Michigan to correlate with "warm interpersonal relations as adults,"[3] and was found to have left no negative effects. By incest I do not refer to the "exploration" of naive relatives; I mean the seduction of a younger person by an older for genital pleasure of the older, which typically introduces genital pleasure to the younger as well. Incest thus includes, but is not limited to, hand stimulation, mouth-to-genital contact, anal or coital intercourse. And it is here that the crime is committed against the victim: the naive sexual awareness is exploited, foreclosing normal virginal awakening which sets up healthy, magnetic, life-long bonding. In its place is introduced enormous sexual pleasure. The pleasure becomes addictive, and "since I was used for this, then that is what anybody's body is for: a sexual pleasure machine." And with this, sexual addiction is off and running.

Father-absence. —Elsewhere I have cited some problems which are typical of children who grow up without significant care by their fathers. Effects may often be seen in families where the father is "distant" from the children, either through alcoholism, "workaholism," or other emotional problems. It is enough, here, to recall that boys without fathers are more likely than boys as a group to slip into "macho" behavior or into "inverted" passive homosexual preference. Both abnormalities are more prone to sexual addiction than are boys reared in close contact with "available and warm fathers." The story with girls is the mirror of the confused boys. Girls without fathers do not know how to relate to males in general. Some "act out" their desperation and become sexually aggressive, while their more introverted sisters manage somehow, even through a "wall flower" pattern of behavior, to signal their availability, and they become sexually active and pregnant at virtually the same rate as their more extroverted sisters. Both the passive and the aggressive father-deprived girls are susceptible to the promiscuous, sexually addictive syndrome.[4]

Seduction.—Exactly parallel is any kind of seduction into sexual activity beyond a person's unfolding naive awareness. Mark came to me because his marriage was about to collapse. His wife had been hospitalized over the trauma of his "fornicating episodes." I put the words in quotes because the popular culture describes his messing around more accurately than the people in the Sunday school class he was teaching. His reputation at church was tarnished with rumors of "adultery." When he turned himself in to me, partly pressured by his wife, and partly because he had known and trusted me under other circumstances in another time and place, I took what I call "his sexual history." I began with "first genital contact," then "first ejaculation," then "first intercourse," all with dates and circumstances under which they occurred. I was not prepared for the responses: all occurred at the age of nine. Three neighbor girls, all thirteen, undressed him, tantalized him, then one by one, helped him penetrate them. This occurred several times a month for more than three years, until he started picking out the girls his own age and penetrating them as a regular part of "making out" on after-school casual contacts. He was active with a series of girls into adulthood, into military service, and at age fifty, he continued his sexual addiction. His wife had complained that he was "an animal," always wanting several encounters each day, and simply wearing her out. I reported elsewhere on the male's sexual "appetite,"[5] and how it is developed. In this case, Mark developed an appetite at a rate that ran to some twenty ejaculations per week at its peak, and his marriage was under threat because he was still picking up encounters without any relationship. Mark was robbed of his innocence, and his healthy unfolding bonding process was stolen. Ultimately the meaning of "rape" may take on dimensions larger than sexual assault; Mark lost a great deal more than any technical "virginity." He lost his unique, two-person magnet, and is unlikely ever to experience the strong bonding that comes with innocence unfolding with innocence.

Rape.—By rape, I mean the sexual abuse of anyone in which position, age, status, or mere raw power is the lever by which sexual contact is obtained. Fathers or other adults who use a child for their own sexual purposes are in the same category as predators who stalk women and use physical violence to subdue resistance and make genital contact. And the effects in people I have known are almost exactly the same. There is emotional damage because "I was being used—just like I was a Kleenex or something that could be thrown away." This "used object" syndrome expresses itself when a woman describes herself as a "slut," a "whore," or a "thing." I have often heard these self-labels from women who took no initiative for sexual intimacy and who were in a powerless position when the abuse or rape was occurring. Yet, as adult women, they "feel like" objects instead of persons. If you complicate this pathological low self-esteem with elements of poverty and hunger, you have the ingredients for prostitution for "bread" or money, and the sex organs then become tools for one's support. While most often this tragedy comes to women, it is by no means limited to one sex. One student of mine dropped out of seminary, experienced first one failure, then another, and eventually was "hired" by a wealthy widow to be her world-traveling attendant, primarily for sexual use. It was ten years before he managed to return to integrity and deal with the original source of the destruction of his self-esteem.

Peer points.—Phil, at thirteen, was six feet tall. He had preferences for older friends. They were "fast lane" juniors

and seniors in high school and may have talked more sex
than they knew. He was tantalized by their talk of intercourse, and they urged him to "do it." Phil told me how
he got up the nerve to ask a girl in his general science
class if she had ever had sex. She hadn't, but was interested.
They conspired to "do it" on a Friday when teachers were
at a convention. Phil's mother introduced him to me. She
had suggested that we talk, and had told me that she knew
something was up on that Friday morning. Phil had spent
too much time in the shower, had left the house dressed
much too well for a day off. But he returned before noon,
crying and shattered. He blurted the truth out to his father.
The whole thing had gone badly. Phil went into some kind
of emotional depression and eventually had a year of therapy. Then, at sixteen, he ran away. His parents were relieved after a few weeks to find that he had turned up at
a Catholic "half-way house." He was both sexually addictive
and deeply dependent on drugs by this time. Phil was innocent, sensitive, and obviously naively endowed with a capacity for exclusive bonding. He wanted so much to win the
approval of his cool friends that he paid a very high price,
only to find that he had not sufficiently deadened his sensitivity on the way.

Pornography.—Phil's friends had deadened their sensitivity to their own sexual gifts by a small career of obsceni-
ties, jokes, and explicit sex magazines and movies. The
"rehearsal" of exploitation through such stimulation sets
the stage for dehumanizing all other people along with
the self, and seeing them as mere objects for sexual use.
Ironically, this "main stream" injection of "porn" tends
to produce the slowly desensitized fornicator: harlot,
whoremonger, prostitute, and pimp. Today, they tend not
to be "doing it" for money, but for other instrumental exchanges: marijuana for sex, "coke" for sex, a Big Mac for
sex. Sometimes a bumper sticker states the terms of the
instrumental exchange: "Marijuana for Sex!" And the adult
versions all look the same. Life revolves around the next
sexual climax. People are useful only if they are able to
give pleasure. But the ironic twist comes when their sexual
fires go out.

Sexual communication among adults tends to decline in cultures in which pornography flourishes. The so-called "sex magazines" turn out to be, in fact, "anti-sex," and the sexual activity in such a culture appears to go into decline.[6] Print and movie pornography tends to trap males more often than females. It would be easy to believe that males are more "visually" oriented than females, but the evidence is less clear than we need to make that assertion. What we do know is that the male's "hydraulic" sex system and the exterior genitals keep him more aware of his sexual feelings than the typical female is. His ejaculation pattern, once begun, will continue, and his psychosocial sexual appetite tends to be fully developed within thirty-six months after that first ejaculation.[7] The "porn" market, therefore, exploits this normal development of male sexuality, with the tragic effect that addiction to pornography tends to desensitize the male, such that a bonded heterosexual relationship is not only unlikely to develop, but the genuine relationship with one exclusive person is not even desired.

The sexual addiction trap tends to make the predator restless, even in the presence of the finest potential relationship in the world. "I don't know why I treated her so shabbily," one broken sexual predator told me. "God could not have created a more beautiful, loving, and good woman than Judy. And I treated her like she was garbage."

Sex for love.—"If you love me, you will make love to me tonight," is innocent enough and may even sound or feel like "true love." But more sexual addiction today is planted in the naive and unprotected "young love" sequence than in any other. David Elkind, in his *All Grown Up and No Place to Go*, reports that only ten percent of high school girls were sexually active twenty years ago, compared to fifty percent today. "The media and merchandisers, too, no longer abide by the unwritten rule that teen-agers are a privileged group who require special promotion and nurturing. They now see teen-agers as fair game for all the arts of persuasion and sexual innuendo once directed only at adult audiences and consumers."[8]

If anyone begins to turn green for envy of the sexual privileges of today's young, save some energy to weep. Even

teen-age intercourse that escapes the horrors of pregnancy
or abortion or both, tends to launch the young person into
a series of increasingly "fast" relationships. Dale, thirty-five,
wept for his troubled marriage. "At fifteen," he said, "I
was in love. We had sex all the time. I thought I would
marry Elyse. But I was drafted. She started sleeping around.
I came home and married Alene, and we have a lot to be
happy about."

"What happened to Elyse?"

"She is still on the prowl—twenty years later. She has
been through three brief marriages, but she has slept with
dozens of men. She still lives near here, and I am stabbed
with guilt whenever I think of her. I turned her on to all
of that, and she has gone crazy with it."

Even the *Redbook* report on 100,000 women discovered
much the same thing: early sexual experience tended to
correlate with (1) dissatisfaction with their present marriages, (2) unhappiness with the level of sexual intimacy,
and (3) low self-esteem. On the other hand, women who
had been intimate only with their husbands ranked highest
of all groups on all three factors, and, besides, showed the
lowest scores on having had an affair outside of their
marriages.[9]

Masturbation.—Most masturbation, both in males and females, is not an indication of "sexual addiction." While masturbation may indeed increase the sexual appetite, it tends
not to correlate with promiscuity or sexual addiction, even
in the form of long-term masturbation. Masturbatory addiction tends to show up in cases characterized by: (1) lowering
interest in social contact, (2) depression, (3) isolation, and
(4) immobilization of vocational or recreational ideals.

Matt came to me early in his senior year, and signed in
for an appointment. "I transferred here from Gordon, so
I have only been here one year. But I am desperate. I can't
go into ministry until I get help," he began. "And I want
to talk to you for two reasons. I have watched you now
for three semesters, and I think I trust you. But I have
also come to you because you don't know me, and I will
probably never see you again after I graduate in May."

"That's OK," I said, "but if you unload something painful

to you, and if I become involved in your solution, we may be stuck with each other, much as 'blood brothers' are. Are you willing to risk that?"

Matt recently told me that he was so frightened that he has no memory of that opening exchange. His masturbation was dragging him down. He was into his third year of marriage. He would masturbate once or twice each day in their apartment, sometimes never leaving to attend class or to study. He was unable to perform with his wife most of the time.

"Honesty is the way out," I told Matt. "Your wife will be your strong partner to walk you through this battle. Besides, she deserves to know how much sexual energy you have—it all belongs to her." Matt's eager search for help led him to a positive view of his sexuality. And his wife was more than willing to be his partner in reconstruction. Now, many years later, they are occasional house guests in our home. But when I was doing a series of lectures on the campus where he is the pastor of College Church, I saw the heavy counseling traffic at his office each afternoon.

"You can probably guess what a lot of them come to unload on me," he said. He was remembering that I once said to him in an early session, "When you are out of the woods on this problem, you will have an indelible sign across your forehead. It will say, 'I am safe. I have struggled and survived.' "

Most adolescent masturbation tends to be "rehearsal" for the "real thing," and this characteristic extends even to "same sex" mutual masturbation. Beyond adolescence, masturbation tends to be supplemental to marital intercourse, and rarely defrauds the intimacy with the spouse where healthy communication and affection are present.

Homosexual contact.—While most mutual masturbation among the young involves "same sex" exploration, it is typically not addictive and is not targeted on homosexual preference. And where it occurs between peers, the exploration is almost universally "heterosexually" targeted, and is driven by the motor of anticipation of heterosexual intercourse at some future time. With these conditions, a typical "friendship bond" tends to develop which remains strong and healthy. That relationship tends to extend from a single encounter up to three years of absorbing friendship accompanied by genital experience. Among the homosexually oriented sexual addicts with whom I have worked, there is a single thread. They tend to have been "used" by an older person who obviously had a great deal of experience seducing younger men. Yet the status of the relationship was such that it was sustained by "instrumental" rewards or threats. This older person then terminated the relationship, and the young man was in the vacuum of needing a close human relationship to replace the dependency. Since the victim had never been responsible for developing a social relationship, he typically went directly for genital contact, often with others he had known to be sexually used in the same context.

Homosexual addicts, often with highly developed frequency patterns, tend to quickly become promiscuous. They typically move to "one-night-stand" operations of the gay bar variety, even though they do not drink, and may accumulate several hundred partners in a few years. "For a while I used to want to know who my partner was, then I remember making contact on a beach in Florida, one time, and going to his apartment for the night. But I remember telling him I did not want to know anything about him, not even his name, so we used nicknames for the evening," one homosexual addict told me.

Joe had first been used by an athlete at the Christian college he attended. It was a great boost to his ego, but the athlete broke it off with him, and Joe phoned the "hotline" for sexual problems in the city where his college was located. They promised to put him in touch with help. Within an hour he was in the private limousine of an Episcopal priest who was to "help him." The help consisted of a one-night homosexual encounter, and the promiscuity was spawned.

Lesbian seduction and addiction appears to be a significantly smaller problem than homosexual seduction and addiction. Physiologically, females do not have the "motor" of a hydraulic system behind sexual pleasure, and affectively, females tend to place relationships more consistently ahead of pleasure. But again, there are notable exceptions within both sexes to these consistent generalizations. I have wanted here to cite typical paths into sexual addiction. But I am more eager now to say that there is nothing inevitable about moving into fornication and promiscuity. Many of us would avoid "like the plague" any early pattern that might foreclose opportunities for lifelong wholeness in human relationships.

Lewdness: The Tragedy beyond Fornication

There seems to be one step further out from sanity in the sexual addiction end of the human intimacy spectrum. It is described in the metaphoric story of God's love affair with Israel. You may remember that God found Israel as a baby kicking in her blood, abandoned. He saved her life, cared for her, and when her sexual maturity blossomed, he "spread the corner of my garment over you and covered your nakedness." God married Israel. But she committed adultery against God, then slipped into prostitution, and finally, God asks, "Did you not add lewdness to all your other detestable practices?"

> You adulterous wife! You prefer strangers to your own husband! Every prostitute receives a fee, but you give gifts to all your lovers, bribing them to come to you from everywhere for your illicit favors. So in your prostitution you are the opposite of others; no one runs after you for your favors. You are the very opposite, for you give payment and none is given to you.
>
> Ezekiel 16:32–34

This aggressive, "on the make" characteristic shows up in the inappropriate gifts of clothing, flowers, dinner dates, which simply do not match the time or affectional investment either person has put into the relationship. If this deformed "affectional" behavior is more typically characteristic of "lewd" women, parallel to the Ezekiel description, there may be another more typically "sex appropriate" male form of lewdness. Both forms of sexual addiction and lewdness amount to a gradual desensitization of the gift of human bonding.

Males tend to go "one step beyond" mere promiscuity as they descend down a ladder of sexual addiction which moves from naive experimentation to promiscuity, bisexuality, sometimes bestiality, child sexual abuse, sadism, and finally violence.

One of the more obscure stories from the Old Testament tells of a Levite from Ephraim who took a concubine from Bethlehem in Judah. She was sexually unfaithful to him, ran away, and returned home. The Levite went after her, and returning, they had to stop overnight in Gibeah. There, an Ephraimite living in Gibeah learned that the Levite and his concubine planned to spend the night on the street with their animals. The resident cautioned against such a decision and brought the Levite and the concubine into the house.

> While they were enjoying themselves, some of the wicked men of the city surrounded the house. Pounding on the door, they shouted to the old man who owned the house, "Bring out the man who came to your house so we can have sex with him."
>
> The owner of the house went outside and said to them, "No, my friends, don't be so vile. Since this man is my guest, don't do this disgraceful thing. Look, here is my virgin daughter, and his concubine. I will bring them out to you now, and you can use them and do to them whatever you wish. But to this man, don't do such a disgraceful thing."
>
> But the men would not listen to him. So the man took his concubine and sent her outside to them, and they raped her and abused her throughout the night, and at dawn they let her go. At daybreak the woman went back to the house where her master was staying, fell down at the door and lay there until daylight.
>
> When her master got up in the morning and opened the door of the house and stepped out to continue on his way, there lay his concubine, fallen in the doorway of the house, with her hands on the threshold. He said to her, "Get up; let's go." But there was no answer. Then the man put her on his donkey and set out for home.
>
> When he reached home, he took a knife and cut up his concubine, limb by limb, into twelve parts and sent them into all the areas of Israel. Everyone who saw it said, "Such a thing has never been seen or done, not since the day the Israelites came up out of Egypt. Think about it! Consider it! Tell us what to do!"
>
> Judges 19:22–30

This horror story comes from a period when "there was no king in Israel" and "everyone did what was right in their own eyes." The comparison between such an environment and the present permissive culture is striking.

In the mid-1970s, it was widely reported that a violent sex movie was circulating underground in the United States. It was allegedly shot in South America, and some half-dozen prints were reportedly smuggled here. In the film, a gang of men rape an attractive young woman, climaxing with the meat cleaver murder of the woman. She was cut up while yet living, even more sadistic than the concubine carving from Judges 19. But since sexual promiscuity leads to sexual addiction, the fading response to one stimulus sets the stage for some more exotic stimulus down the road. We can easily echo the postscript: "Think about it! Consider it! Tell us what to do!"[10]

In a United Press International news release circulated in March of 1985, the headline ran: "Hefner suffers stroke, opts for new philosophy." Hugh Hefner, founder of the famous *Playboy* enterprises, was quoted as saying,

"I survived a stroke two weeks ago," Hefner, 59, said in a statement. "My recovery is total and something of a miracle. What has happened is actually a 'stroke of luck' that I fully expect will change the direction of my life."

In the statement, Hefner blamed the stroke on stress caused by Peter Bogdanovich's book about the murder of the 1980 Playmate of the Year, *The Killing of the Unicorn: Dorothy Stratten 1960–1980*. The book suggests that Hefner "lured Stratten into a Hollywood lifestyle that resulted in her death." If Bogdanovich's confessions for himself and Hefner in their contribution to her violent death bear any resemblance to the truth, then the *Playboy* mansion in Los Angeles has been the setting for jacuzzi pool parties with group sex, sodomy, and bestiality involving famous and named participants who did sexual acts with collie dogs.[11]

As the *Playboy* intrigue continues to break in mid-1985, the *Chicago Tribune* reports with a headline: "Centerfold being shifted at *Playboy*." Christie Hefner, Hugh's daughter and "corporation chief," reports: "It's the end of an era, but the problem always was that we had to work our quality fiction and writing around the centerfold." The *Tribune* chronicled the origin of *Playboy*, peaking and then winding down with:

> Hefner, by his own proud admission, shared intimate hours with many centerfolds; he preached the philosophy of health through hedonism. And writer Gay Talese called the centerfold "a sensational focal point" and pegged Hefner as "the first man to become rich by openly mass marketing masturbatory love through the illusion of an available alluring woman."
>
> But today, the man in the bathrobe is recovering from a stress-induced stroke. His private DC-9 with the shower and round bed covered in Tasmanian fur has been sold to the Venezuelan government. Circulation [of *Playboy*] has plummeted by nearly 3 million readers, from a high of 6.9 million in 1972. The [*Playboy*] clubs are nearly gone. And the Chicago [*Playboy*] mansion is now an art school.
>
> Bad management had hurt the company, but, more important, readers had become numb to the novelty of nudity.
>
> "In a sense," said *Playboy* publicity chief Dennis Salyers, "we worked ourselves out of a job. At one time, we were on the leading edge of sexual change in this country. Nowadays, nobody here would want to be on the leading edge of sexual change because it would mean doing it with kangaroos or something."[12]

There you have it: "the leading edge of sexual change" has now arrived at bestiality, "doing it with kangaroos. . . ." It is odd that he didn't mention collie dogs.

When I think of the desensitization of the finer human values, I recall once reading that John Wesley's mother wrote a "rule" for her Oxford student son, by which he might "judge the lawfulness or unlawfulness of any pleasure." Here it is:

> Whatever weakens your reason,
> impairs the tenderness of your conscience,
> obscures your sense of God, or
> takes off your relish of spiritual things;
> in short,
> whatever increases the strength

and authority of your body over your mind,
that thing is sin to you,
however innocent it may be in itself.

Some Ways Back from Promiscuity

Enough bad news. The good news is that God who has created all things "good" can make all things "new" through Jesus. I wish now to turn to list some of the strategies and paths which are signals of hope to those who are themselves trapped in sexual addiction. But these markers also may encourage those of us who stand close to people who seem out of control: a spouse, a son or daughter, even a parent.

Education for holiness.—The story everywhere is the same. A nineteen-year-old coed at Lycoming College says, "I always hoped something like this was true, but why didn't anybody tell us? If I had known how God made us, I would not have had an abortion at sixteen." In a large Ohio church, Sunday morning, a seventeen-year-old senior says, "Why weren't you the preacher last Sunday morning? If you had told me then what you told us just now, I would not have had intercourse with my girlfriend this week. I could have waited until marriage, but nobody ever told me anything like that before."

The wall plaques about who the head of this house is, and how to find the desires of your heart may have been enough to inspire my generation. But today's homes are assaulted by sexual seduction from almost every side. Our silence as parents and as congregations leaves our young to infer: nobody cares; it's OK; and everybody's doing it.

Friendship commitment.—Significant friendships in which each of several persons looks out for the welfare of the others are probably our best guarantee, apart from God's grace, of keeping our sanity and keeping a perspective on values that matter most. In his famous "eight steps of reality therapy," William Glasser outlines a strategy that evolves almost instinctually where relationships are based on mutual respect.

1. Establish a basis for friendship and explore, "What is it that you want, really want?"

2. Inquire: What are you doing now that is likely to give you what you really want?

3. Is what you are doing helping or hindering?

4. Can I help you explore options and make a plan for getting what you want?

5. Are you ready to let me check you out regularly on your progress, so you can revise your plan and make it work?

6. [Don't accept excuses.]

7. [Don't punish, but don't interfere with reasonable consequences, and don't criticize.]

8. [Never give up.][13]

Glasser's scheme rests squarely on principles Jesus used with people. Jesus never went scrambling after somebody to buttonhole them and drag them to commitment. He would help them to explore the options, offer to "contract" for obedience to a plan, but left the choosing to the individual.

Loving enough to let go.—There is a strange, twice-repeated statement in St. Paul. It plays a theme of "releasing such a person to Satan."

> When you are assembled in the name of our Lord Jesus and I am with you in spirit, and the power of our Lord Jesus is present, hand this man over to Satan, so that the sinful nature [flesh] may be destroyed and his spirit saved on the day of the Lord.
>
> 1 Corinthians 5:4–5

> Timothy, my son, I give you this instruction in keeping with the prophecies once made about you, so that by following them you may fight the good fight, holding on to faith and a good conscience. Some have rejected these and so have shipwrecked their faith. Among them are Hymenaeus and Alexander, whom I have handed over to Satan to be taught not to blaspheme.
>
> 1 Timothy 1:18–20

I first seriously considered this repeated teaching by Paul when I was reading Margie Lewis's book, *The Hurting Parent.*[14] In it one couple, deeply distraught over their daughter's rebellion, seemed drawn to this repugnant teaching. It seemed to be a turning point in the relationship with the alienated child.

Look at major lines of reasoning that are present in the passage: (1) Persons choose whom they will serve; no one else makes that choice; hence "releasing" or "handing over" is not punishment, but recognition that a choice has been made. (2) The "prince of this world" is already surrounding those who are in rebellion against God and truth. (3) In the case of the sexually addicted, fornicating person, the "release" may denote the liberation of the parent or spouse: neurotic efforts to control other adults against their will may be almost as addictive as fornication. (4) The "handing over" was specifically to allow natural consequences to be hastened in the hopes that grace would ultimately triumph and these lost people would come home to truth and health. Hymenaeus and Alexander were "handed over" so they could learn not to "blaspheme." This was unlikely a matter of obscene words, but whatever the tendency, its correction needed to "run its course" and produce its harvest in the hopes that they would be "taught" or corrected.[15]

Coming home under their own steam.—The famous story of the gentle father and the prodigal son illustrates how important it is to so respect the rebelling adult that the return home is at the initiative of the one who chose to leave. Sometimes a smothering home even contributes to the "flight syndrome" of young prodigals. But whatever the reason, "tying a yellow ribbon around the old oak tree" and glancing down the street in the hopes of seeing a familiar form turning toward home are appropriate impulses for the unconditionally loving spouse or parent or child. Tough love insists that, barring physical or mental disability, it is important to let everyone feel the full weight of moral responsibility.

When they crash and burn.—We are always ready to take responsibility for those who lose control, who need hospitalization or suicide prevention counseling. "I had heard other guys say that their parents would 'kill them' if they knew what they were doing. But I knew it would break my parents' hearts. I might 'kill them' with my choices, but they would not kill me."

Repentance.—Humiliation and shame almost never lead to moral change or Christian conversion. "Godly sorrow" is "coming home to the truth." Embarrassment is a device for protecting the self, but guilt is the motive for putting things right with other significant relationships: "I have sinned against God and against you," denotes repentance. So, when a young man was in tears pacing my living room floor saying, "I'm so embarrassed," I held off and simply said, "Calm down now, let's see what your options are. I'm going to stick with you and see you through this." Only later was I able to bring him to repentance. Godly sorrow then prompted him to grieve and repent of his sin against his girlfriend of three years whom he infected with a disease that he picked up from a one-night stand with a former high school friend who propositioned and nailed him for instrumental sex. The untimely bond was eventually lost as well, and three years of grief and healing with no dating at all saw him grounded in personal integrity and ready for a significant relationship again.

A curriculum for renewal.—"Tell me how the promiscuous sexual addict can come home again and start over," I said to my "Discipleship Development in the Home" class recently.

"Well, I would begin by helping as many people to understand how the bonding capacity gets damaged by promiscuity. I don't think most people even think about that as a possibility. And even with people who are badly damaged, I think they need to know what has gone wrong."

"Time. That's what I think. They've got to go through a kind of 'detox' period, so they can re-charge their sexual magnet if they are going to get healed. Yet most of these folks go right from one intimacy to another. It's no wonder they used to kill sexual predators, like it says in Deuteronomy 22."

"People. They've got to have significant relationships that are not romantic. Your 'trampoline' idea from *Bonding* applies here. In fact, I imagine most promiscuous people have almost a lifelong deficit in affection and touch. And if they are going to get well, they've got to have safe people around them."

"I worry about 'singles' groups' in the churches. I've known people who were consistently hustled toward bed by people out of conservative, even Bible church kinds of singles' clubs. I wonder if they are much safer than singles' bars, especially if they are known as 'match-maker singles' ministries. I think the formerly promiscuous person needs healthy people, both single and married, in their support network."

Perhaps this is a curriculum of sorts. I've been told by victims of sexually promiscuous addicts working in the church that we need some symbol, maybe even an insignia, a bracelet, or a pendant that expresses in some clear but sensitive way the sentiment so many people feel: "We need time before intimacy again. I need people, but not sexual advances."

When Mother Teresa spoke at Harvard in the early 1980s, the crowd of students went breathless as this shriveled up Christian giant said, "I am told that some of you are having premarital sex. And I hear that some of you even are getting abortions. I must tell you that this is wrong." If most of us had tried pronouncing such judgments on a university crowd today we might have been jeered. It takes a certain kind of authority and an unconditional commitment to love if we are going to make direct confrontation of evil.

Mother Teresa, whom I have not met, reminds me, however, of Julia Shelhamer, whose ministry with the poor, the blacks, and the drunks extended wherever she lived: Shreveport; Washington, D.C.; Winona Lake, Indiana; Wilmore, Kentucky. Our lives overlapped in her last two decades at her final two locations.

Dr. J. F. Gregory once asked Mrs. Shelhamer, in her early eighties, how she liked living at Winona Lake, compared to Washington, D.C., from which she had just moved. "I like it very well," she said, "but I miss the drunks." She had listed what may well have been the first "dial-a-prayer" in her Washington, D.C. days. She was the live "pray-er" for those who called her at all hours of the day and night.

When I learned that she was making regular Thursday afternoon visits to local bars in northern Indiana, I asked her what she did when she walked into a bar or lounge.

"Oh, Doctor Joy, a younger woman could not do what I do. First, I always ask the proprietor whether I may speak to some of his patrons. Not one has ever refused me." I could understand that. Who could refuse this withered woman who weighed less than ninety pounds? "Then, I look for some man who is sitting alone and drinking. I walk to his table or climb on the seat next to him, and I ask him, 'Do you have a mother?' "

I was in shock. How could a man say, "No"? It was a truly universal question. It was non-adversarial. And it opened what is likely a critical agenda for emotionally crippled and dependent men.

Welcome Home, Virgins!

There is a scene in *Man of LaMancha* where Don Quixote salutes Aldonza, a prostitute, calling her "My virgin!" This fantasy evokes a violent response in her extended solo. Quixote has changed her name from Aldonza to Dulcinea, as he changes her reputation from that of a whore to a whole and pure woman. The elegance of the musical is signaled by its theme song, "The Impossible Dream."

And it seems an impossible dream when God, the Lover, pursues Israel, the "wife," as she prostitutes her faithfulness by worshiping heathen gods with all sorts of immoral worship practices. And it is an impossible dream that drives Hosea in pursuit of his wife Gomer as she is "on the make" with all sorts of temporary lovers. In both cases, the ultimate goal is to pursue the unfaithful spouse until she returns to her virginal state. Ultimately, God transforms the reputation of Israel back from harlot to virgin:

"Sing, O barren woman, you who never bore a child; . . .
Do not be afraid; you will not suffer shame.
    Do not fear disgrace; you will not be humiliated.
You will forget the shame of your youth
    And remember no more the reproach of your widowhood.
For your Maker is your husband—
    The Lord Almighty is his name—
The Holy One of Israel is your redeemer;

He is called the God of all the earth.
The Lord will call you back
   As if you were a wife deserted and distressed in spirit
A wife who married young, only to be rejected,"
Says your God.

Isaiah 54:1, 5–6

No longer will they call you Deserted
   Or name your land Desolate.
But you will be called Hephzibah,
   And your land Beulah;
For the Lord will take delight in you,
   And your land will be married.
As a young man marries a maiden,
   So will your sons marry you;
As a bridegroom rejoices over his bride,
   So will your God rejoice over you.

Isaiah 62:4–5

The Lord appeared to us in the past, saying:
"I have loved you with an everlasting love;
   I have drawn you with loving-kindness.
I will build you up again
   And you will be rebuilt, O Virgin Israel. . . .
Set up road signs; put up guideposts.
   Take note of the highway, the road that you take.
Return, O Virgin Israel, return to your towns.
   How long will you wander, O unfaithful daughter?
The Lord will create a new thing on earth—
   A woman will surround [protect] a man."

Jeremiah 31:3–4, 21–22

In the Old Testament, God demanded a kind of physical perfection as a human metaphor of his own perfection in Deity. The priests might not have any physical imperfection, indeed no man could enter the Temple if he had an amputation or an undescended testicle. No imperfect animal could be used in making a sacrifice. No menstruating woman might have social contact of any kind; even her husband could not touch her. All of these "screening" criteria seem to focus on using physical wholeness to bear witness to the wholeness and holiness of God.

But in the New Testament, the perfect Son has come to represent the perfect Father. The burden of being a "perfect human specimen" seems forever to have been lifted. Indeed, Jesus was defaced, humiliated, and denuded in full public view, only to destroy the power of evil and destruction by rising from the dead on the third day.

Matthew's Gospel opens with an extended, but by no means complete, genealogy of Jesus. Only five women appear. One is Tamar, who used the guise of prostitution to entrap Judah, her father-in-law, to raise up an heir in behalf of her dead husband. Another is Rahab, the harlot, who housed the spies before the Israelites entered Palestine. A third is Ruth, the Gentile daughter of Naomi, both of whom were widows, victims of famine. But Ruth's marriage to Boaz produced a son who entered the genealogy of Jesus. The fourth was the mother of Solomon. She "had been Uriah's wife." Bathsheba is so named in the text, no doubt, to allow history to witness that this woman (taken from her husband through adultery and his arranged murder by King David, though defiled and imperfect) is a bona fide "carrier" of God's purposes. Mary, the mother of Jesus, is the final woman named in Matthew's genealogy; she was in the embarrassing social position of being pregnant before her marriage and without the knowledge or assistance of her betrothed husband.

It is a new day. Not only do the heathen, the promiscuous, and the adulterous win acceptance in the future, even the genealogy with its backward look redeems them. Not only are they redeemed, they are also memorialized, as if to serve notice to all future troubled people: there is hope for you!

The apostle Paul was possibly a widower of some sort, since membership in the Jewish Sanhedrin was limited to married Jewish males with impeccable credentials. And Jesus cites for the twelve disciples conditions under which celibacy might be possible:

> Not everyone can accept this teaching, but only those to whom it has been given. For some are eunuchs because they were born that way; others were made that way by men; and others

have made themselves eunuchs because of the kingdom of heaven. The one who can accept this should accept it.

Matthew 19:11–12

"Eunuchs" were males whose reproductive capacity was missing. Some had "birth defects," Jesus suggests, hence would not have the motivation for "one-flesh" marital bonding. Others were literally "made that way by the surgeon's knife." They had been castrated, as in the case of some household slaves. But others may sacrifice the sexual energy in the service of God's work on earth. Notice how radically different this acceptance is compared with the Levitical prohibitions for the priests:

[Priests] must not marry women defiled by prostitution or divorced from their husbands, because priests are holy to their God. Regard them as holy, because they offer up the food of your God. Consider them holy, because I the Lord, who makes you holy, am holy. . . . For the generations to come none of your descendants who has a defect may come near to offer the food of his God. No man who has any defect may come near; no man who is blind or lame, disfigured or deformed; no man with a crippled foot or hand, or who is hunchbacked or dwarfed, or who has any eye defect, or who has festering or running sores or damaged testicles. No descendant of Aaron the priest who has any defect is to come near to present the offerings made to the Lord by fire.

Leviticus 2:7–8, 17–21

How does Jesus set aside the "perfectionistic" standards for the priesthood when he is calling the apostles? How does he violate the priestly regulations in his social contact? Nowhere is Jesus more in confrontation with reasonable cultural expectations than when a "sinful woman" crashes the party at the house of Simon the Pharisee. Was she Mary of Magdala? Was she a harlot, a woman of the street? Simon finds himself talking to himself:

"If this man were a prophet, he would know who is touching him and what kind of woman she is—that she is a sinner."
Jesus answered him, "Simon, I have something to tell you."

"Tell me, teacher," he said.

"Two men owed money to a certain moneylender. One owed him five hundred denarii, and the other fifty. Neither of them had the money to pay him back, so he canceled the debts of both. Now which of them will love him more?"

Simon replied, "I suppose the one who had the bigger debt canceled."

"You have judged correctly," Jesus said. Then he turned toward the woman and said to Simon, "Do you see this woman? I came into your house. You did not give me a kiss, but this woman, from the time I entered, has not stopped kissing my feet. You did not put oil on my head, but she has poured perfume on my feet. Therefore, I tell you, her many sins have been forgiven—for she loved much. But he who has been forgiven little loves little."

Then Jesus said to her, "Your sins are forgiven."

Luke 7:39–48

The pattern is clear. The way back begins with acceptance and affirmation. The deficits in esteem are so enormous in the sexually addicted that they are hopelessly trapped in egocentric shame and humiliation. They may seem to be arrogant, rude, aggressive, and obscene, but these are most often window dressing to hide the crushed, all-but-annihilated inner self.

Robbie and I sat with Mack in our library from 3:30 in the morning until daylight. He was suicidal, homicidal, and drunk. We laced him with coffee. He had phoned at half-past midnight to say "Good-bye" ready to move from the pay phone in Lexington first to shoot his estranged wife, then himself. I kept him on the line for an hour and a half.

"Mack, I'm going to make a decision for you," I said.

"You have no right to make a decision for me!"

"If I were in as bad shape as you are, you would make a decision for me, and I would want you to do it. Let me tell you what you are going to do. I'm going upstairs when I hang up. I'm going to make up a bed for you. You are going to get in your pickup and drive to Wilmore."

He finally agreed to come. That meant that the door to suicide was closed. "But," he said, "I have some business to take care of first. So I won't ring your doorbell. You will find me in the truck in your driveway in the morning when you get up."

I dispatched the Lexington police to his wife's address, then I phoned the Wilmore police asking them to notify me when his pickup hit the city limits. My phone rang in time for me to call the Lexington police to notify them that the lapsed time indicated he had not gone to his wife's address. Then I walked out to bring him in.

By five o'clock, Robbie and I had sobered him up and had him walking us through his childhood. We literally held on to him, one of us holding each of his hands while he talked. He was the youngest child in a large, nominally Catholic family in Bardstown, Kentucky. Both parents were deeply alcoholic. Weeks would pass, he said, in which his father would not speak to him, but would only strike him.

From the age of fifteen, Mack had been promiscuous, losing count of the one-night stands from pick-ups at singles' bars. Now we sat with this construction contractor in our home. Almost spontaneously, at first, we began a litany of adoption:

"I wish we had been there, Mack, to hold you when you were a baby. We could have touched you, laughed with you, wiped your tears when you cried.

"When you started to school, we could have followed your progress, been proud of you, and helped you fight your battles with friends and teachers, if you needed that.

"We would have wanted to meet your 'first girl,' and to share the excitement of your first real love relationship.

"And in Vietnam, we would have prayed for you, worried ourselves sick for you, and have come to you when you were brought in after two days of lying face-down in the mud, full of shrapnel that messed up your legs and arms.

"But we have you now, after thirty-four years, we finally found you, and we will never let you go."

So we hugged and cried. It may have opened a new chapter for Mack. Next June, I received a phone call asking me to stand by for a call coming in from the Philippines.

"It's me—Mack. I had to sign up for a 'Father's Day call' two weeks ago, and even then, it had to be on a Thursday. But I wanted to talk to you. It seemed important to me."

There are a dozen other stories with the same plot line.

The details are different. Mack's story is still in process. We took some risks with him, but they were ones worth taking, regardless of the outcome.

In this chapter I have assaulted you with the evidence that sexual promiscuity/addiction is a tragic perversion of what may well be the grandest gift to humans: the gift of exclusive and intimate lifelong bonding, the ultimate pinnacle expression of God's gift of "community." Remember: "It is not good for the human to be alone"? I want you to come away from this glimpse of obscenity—which is as close as your newsstand—ready to look the promiscuous sexual addicts in the face and see them as God always sees them: as potential "virgins," capable of healing and restoration by the grace of Jesus.

QUESTIONS PEOPLE ASK

Q: What happens if you find you are married to a person who has been, and continues to be, promiscuous? Shouldn't you leave that person?

A: No one would blame you much if you left. Yet you are likely "bonded" to the promiscuous person, though that person is likely unable to bond with anyone at this time. If you choose to be faithful to the unfaithful one, you will have made an unconditional, loving choice. And it will take unusual courage and grace to live out your decision. But if you can do it, and if you can affirm the other person, and express belief that they will one day come around, the probabilities are good that you will see them healed. Time is on your side. Promiscuity tends to wane at midlife. A loving and faithful spouse may expect to see fidelity arrive finally. It may look like God's pursuit of unfaithful Israel or Hosea's fidelity to fornicating Gomer. But it is a courageous and grace-filled adventure, should you choose it.

Q: What about people in the "sex business"—massage parlors, topless dancers, and people who pose nude for the centerfolds and calendars? Are they fornicators? I'm having trouble getting used to using that word in your new way.

A: Right on! But I am only using the word fornicator exactly as the Bible consistently uses it. It is the very same root word as gets translated prostitute, whore, harlot, whoremonger. Remember? So, yes. These people are fornicators. But we will need to see them as God sees them, and that is as people trapped in sexual addiction. So their "deliverance" must follow a pattern quite different from that needed by "adulterers," who are basically healthy people whose bond has been stretched to cover an alien as well as the primary love relationship. If you should read Dorothy Stratten's story (see footnote 3 of chapter 3 for the citation) you will weep as you see her seduced by a man who simply wanted to rape her and to get her photograph, with which he wanted to win a place in Hugh Hefner's inner circle. She burst into tears at every photography session, and never "got used to it." Another painful but beautifully told story, is that of Gypsy Rose Lee, as told by her son, Erik Lee Preminger, in *Gypsy and Me.* Gypsy's is the classical story of the father-absent, desperate girl who "sells her body" in seductive stage displays as a strip-tease artist.

Erik tells how she selected his natural father intentionally so that she would have someone—a baby—no one could ever take away from her. Here is the typical but tragic, "instrumental use" of a baby by a woman who is willing to settle for a baby if she cannot get her man. She was crushed, at the time, by the break-up of a sexual alliance with the famous Mike Todd, who left her for another paramour. *Porneia,* pornography, and fornication—they are all the same tragic phenomenon. And to this we have the current diagnosis of "sexual addiction." It is easy to see why Deuteronomy 24 and Jesus cite a tragedy which may so seriously flaw a marriage that it cannot survive.

Q: You suggest that boys who are seduced by older same-sex relatives may develop a homosexual appetite. Is the same true for girls and the lesbian preference?

A: I have talked with fewer than a dozen women who indicated a confusion in sexual preference. In none of their histories did we uncover adult incest by a female relative.

The more consistent pattern with lesbian preference seems to be just the opposite. Abuse by an older male, or any other negative experience feeding an attitude of resentment toward males in general, seems more consistently present among active lesbians. Phil Donahue once interrogated the author of *Father's Days* with her parents both on camera with her. The father had used the author sexually when she was a girl in the home. When Donahue raised the question of a possible link between her active lesbian lifestyle and the father incest, she was enraged. It was clear that she thought she was exercising "the right of sexual preference," when, in the more common pattern, she seemed to be living out the orientation of resentment which "generalized" to alienate her affections away from men. If this pattern is, indeed, a prevalent one, it is understandable that a maturing woman would turn to some seemingly safe intimate relationship—and that, not surprisingly, is sometimes with another woman. Remember that the sexual differentiation of the brain sets up the seat of sexual arousal, and the male brain is formed from the female brain configuration, so we tend to see many more problems of sexual orientation with males than with females. I discuss this in chapter 5 of *Bonding: Relationships in the Image of God.* It is entitled "Conception: Differentiating the 'Adam.'"

6

The Tragedy That Stalks Your Very Life

△

My friend Al gathered his family together late one Sunday night. He was then forty-five, with his wife of twenty-three years, and their six children, two married. So, as they huddled there in the living room, wondering what Dad had in mind, Al spoke.

"I need to tell you that for six months I have been sexually involved with Mary. I know you thought she was a good friend of the family. She has showered all of you with gifts. But I have been a fool. And I cannot go on living a lie with you, so today I have told Mary good-bye, and she will not be coming back here and I will not be seeing her again. I don't know quite how it all happened, but I have hidden too much from you, and I want you to know the truth now. I will always tell you the truth."

In the wake of that disclosure, the family was tested to its foundations. Al's wife asked for a few weeks to work through all of this surprise. She flew to Portland to be with her parents while she reorganized her feelings. The children in the home continued to go to school and helped Al keep the household running while Mother was gone.

Now some twenty years later, the marriage has ripened into retirement. The children, all married, are deeply attached to their parents, and the tragedy of adultery seems to have equipped them well for resisting the magnet of an alien bond that might intrude in their own marriages. Unlike sons and daughters of the "adultery and divorce" syndrome where honesty is a price never paid by the failing parents, these sons and daughters have not wavered in their sense of identity, never "acted out" their own sexual adventures in imitation of straying parents, and seem whole and peaceable overall.

Adultery Adulterates

Instead of seeing the word "adultery" as a moralistic label, it may help to look through it to its simple meaning. Drinking water which is adulterated with toxic chemicals is itself poison. A theological value which is compromised with the encroachment of destructive cultural values is an adulterated theology. At its most obvious level, adultery refers to the weakening of one bond by extending the bonding capacity to include another. But there is another possible meaning for "adultery." It moves on the possibility that the "dul" root is related to the Latin word for "sweetness," hence to negate the sweetness with the prefix "a-" would mean "to kill the sweetness" of the relationship.

It is easy to confuse bonding adultery with sexual promiscuity, yet adulterers are distinctly not promiscuous. When a person with high affectional bonding is drawn away into a competing sexual bond, the consistent loving core of the person simply extends the same kind of fidelity to a new lover. These are not "one-night stands," they are deeply grounded love affairs.

So, the adulterated alien bond is still "relational." It still holds persons in high regard and holds the self in high regard. The dagger of bonded love has been driven into the very core of life itself. This is signified in the profoundly executed proverb: "The prostitute reduces you to a loaf of bread, but the adulteress stalks your very life" (Prov. 6:26). When the bond between the virginal bride and groom is "adulterated" by being spread over another bond that is forming, there is only grief and agony that can follow. But the marriage is not necessarily dead. Indeed, the degree or depth of pain that is evoked may be the best indicator of how much hope there is for the survival and recovery of the marriage. If the bond has been allowed to shrivel and wane, there will be little grief if the relationship is put under threat of total loss. So long as there is pain, there is hope for a marriage. Indeed, adultery not only is not "grounds for divorce," it is a signal that a basically healthy personality has experienced disorientation of some tragic sort and has "horned in on" a bond which is a substitute for the original or marital bond. The attention, then, needs to go to restoring the original bond, not in destroying it through legal separation or divorce.

To illustrate all of this, consider Jesus' words in Matthew 19:9—"I tell you that anyone who divorces his wife, except for fornication/harlotry, and marries another woman commits adultery."

For the moment look at the statement with the "exception phrase" temporarily set aside: "I tell you that anyone who divorces his wife . . . and marries another woman commits adultery." Consider that (a) adultery is an effect of divorce, or at least of most of them; and (b) it consists of schizophrenic double bonding. That is, the question here is not merely a moral or legal one, it is a matter of rending the seamless fabric of a marital pair bond. But then, as with the word "murder," an original human tragedy creates the necessity for a moral and legal term. We often get it backward: "Sin is the willful transgression of a known law of God" suggests that the transgression is against a "law." What it misses is the fact that the law came into being not at the whim of God, but to define human tragedy. We, then, are locked into superficiality if we are distressed about "breaking the law." We might, instead, weep for the irreparable damage and the personal anguish denoted by "adultery." It means that one, and more likely two, three, or four hearts have been ripped asunder as a sacred bond was stressed by an alien intruder.

But look again at the omitted phrase:
. . . except for fornication/harlotry . . .
It would appear that there is one condition under which the dissolution of the marriage would not set off a sequence of ripped bonds: the *porneia*/fornication/harlotry

condition. There is no bond, hence no riptide of schizophrenic grief. The fornicating spouse may leave the marriage and be "on the roll" again. Likewise, the faithful and
bonded spouse has likely suffered the repeated grief of the
partner's promiscuity until there is no need for extended
time to mourn and heal, hence no predictable effects of
"adultery."

We might understand these "exception phrases" in Matthew 5 and 19 better if we relocated the phrases after the
adultery caution,

> I tell you that anyone who divorces his wife,
> causes her to commit adultery,
> and anyone who marries a woman so divorced
> commits adultery,
> [except in the case of fornication/harlotry].
>
> Matthew 5:32

We could add, then, "in which case no marital bond is being
adulterated." And here in Matthew 5, it is clear that the
charge of blame is leveled: "causes her to commit adultery."
The divorcer who abandons a marital bond takes responsibility for driving the chisel which divides the schizophrenic
heart. Any spouse thus "put out on the street" is put in
the vulnerable place of accepting an alien bond, with its
predictable schizophrenic trauma which "stalks your very
life."

The Vulnerable Spot

So here we come to the unique responsibility of partners
for each other. David Augsburger tells the story of a man
who was embarrassed publicly for his adultery. He threw
himself onto the mercies of his wife, who was ignorant of
the affair.

> "Forgive you? Of course not. . . ."
> He did not hear the gentleness in her voice. He froze into
> painful silence, then regrets spilled out again. He had betrayed

her trust, the trust of the whole community by becoming sexually intimate with two persons he was committed to help as a skilled counselor.

"No, I will not forgive you. I do not want the kind of relationship with you in which you are the offender and I am the forgiver. I don't want you grateful and indebted to me for the rest of our lives. I want us to work through this until we both understand our parts in the problem, until we can accept each other."[1]

Since adultery specifically implies the ripping of a bond, it necessarily points to two persons who were responsible for the maintenance of the original bond. However much we might want to "blame" the alien bonding person, the partners in the original bond must first be held accountable for any damage or loss.

And since a bond involves two people, neither alone can break the bond. What I am saying here is not true of fornicators—the promiscuous predators who may maintain a marriage for certain convenience, convention, and reproduction benefits, while playing on the side. Promiscuous people may rip through the virginal innocence and health of normally bonding partners, in which case the violence done to the bond may be entirely one-sided. But where the exclusive, monogamous bond was well settled in, either person has many options for enriching, renewing, revitalizing, and otherwise contributing to maintaining and developing a growing bond. Couples do this "dance of life" on a thousand fronts at once: When one is consumed by business, the other manages to breathe life and variation into their schedules by both "knowing the spouse" and knowing the social ticket that will break the tyranny of work. So also, in the sexual arena. They are literally "brother's and sister's keepers." And they know each other so well, know the sexual needs so well, that each partner can look after the affectional and intimate appetites of the other and keep the garden well tended.

"I have reserved Friday night at the Holidome—for our 'Couple Caper' special, complete with recreation facilities, meals, and a king-sized bed," Jerry said as she welcomed Jim home in the middle of a heavy season at the job.

"But what about the kids?"

"I called your Mom and she will pick them up from school."

"You don't know how much work I have to do!"

"Oh, yes I do. But I also know my Jim. And I want to get a tiger in his tank, so he will get 'more miles per gallon' when he works."

Now, that verbal exchange is unlikely for newlyweds. But it is within reach of any couple whose experience and honesty with each other brings the truth down to ground level: how do they work best, what does each need, and who looks out for the other?

Separation.—Brief separations because of travel requirements of the job are not the end of the world for nicely bonded couples. If the traveling spouse is inclined toward promiscuity, then the travel offers variety in the deformed desire to be "on the make." And extended separation of weeks or months can be very stressful even on the best of bonds. St. Paul cautioned that a man and a woman should not be separated except briefly and for good reason: "Do not deprive each other except by mutual consent and for a time, so that you may devote yourselves to prayer. Then come together again so that Satan will not tempt you because of your lack of self-control" (1 Cor. 6:5–6). In the Jewish cycle of taboos, a husband could not touch his wife for approximately two weeks of the month. This "unclean" period provided alternating cycles of intimacy and abstinence, but with the full visual access to each other.

During the early childhood years, it is critical for the young that both parents be available on virtually a daily basis. I deal with this urgency elsewhere.[2] Suffice it to say that the children in a marriage can provide additional "steps" in the pair bonding process, and they draw out elements of *storge, philia,* and *agape* love which enrich the marital bond. So this familial bonding serves to widen the pair bond and its "work agenda" may have in it the strength of steel to see the marriage through the years of stress and into the "empty nest" and retirement phase.

Vocational separation as a "way of life" not only neglects the pair bond, thus potentially weakening it, separation sets up vulnerability for both spouses: one trapped at the home base, and the other moving in a distant world. Each is probably in daily contact with other persons who, sometimes through empathy alone, begin to serve as alternative bonding partners—simply through voice, eye, and occasional light touch contact.

Some of our most public and famous figures "live apart" and hope the spouse "understands." Engelbert Humperdinck and his English wife Pat Dorsey, both in their forties, live apart—partly for immigration and tax reasons. From her Leicester, England, home Pat responds to the paternity suits and the rumors: "I've seen too many stories and too many photographs of him with other women to throw a tantrum now." Of her, London Express Service writer Victor Davis speculates that when she heard the words "with this ring I thee wed" twenty-two years ago, Pat "hadn't realized that the ring in question would more often than not mean a telephone call." Humperdinck tries to shrug off his lover-boy (fornicating) reputation: "Sometimes I feel for Pat. My life does have an open door and I don't know what she thinks about that. I just hope she understands. Cruel people and cruel press have ruined our marriage for months at a time. And Pat does not forget easily. She broods and we can be in a state of suspended animation sometimes for years. The last paternity suit hung over our heads for three years."[3]

Fatigue.—Any form of stress may weaken our bonding with the spouse. But fatigue, exhaustion, and the depletion of an infection or an illness sets up unusual vulnerability. There is a tendency to blame, to whine, to revert to egocentric perspective. All of these tend to reduce us to a childhood state. The marital bond must then shift to *storge* /parental care. And "mothering" or "fathering" may only add to the scenario a dimension of further rejection and anger. When exhaustion depresses sexual interest in the bonded relationship, the affectional needs still lie dormant. Surprisingly enough, they sometimes awaken unpredictably and a bizarre new alliance may suddenly appear. Here, as in so many cases, the physical well-being of the person is a first priority, and caught at a weak point, the surprise may be greatest for the one whose affections are aroused in an alien bond.

Grief.—The affective side of personality, likely centered in the right hemisphere of the brain, is both the center of loving and of other affectional transactions. People who have sustained major losses—the death of a child or a parent, for example—tend to be vulnerable to alien or other inappropriate bonding. Similarly, the grief which follows the loss of a spouse, either through death, divorce, or abandonment, sets up the surviving partner for vulnerability to inappropriate bonding. I cannot stress too much the importance of giving authority to two or three trusted friends for advising when you are ready for social contact again, and in the meantime the personal priority should go to "getting healed" of the traumatic loss you have sustained.

The most frequent violation of "grief" tends to be the quick marriage following a marital or other intimate loss. All of us need acceptance and support when we have suffered the emotional stresses of a break-up or divorce. And when we are "ministered to" by someone who is a potential lover, the two needs tend to blur until we are highly vulnerable to entering a relationship with mixed needs and impaired perception about what either person needs.

Bill was widowed by the death of his wife, and within a month his phone was ringing with "eligible" women inviting him to social contact, long before he should have been ready for dating. Larry's wife first put him under a restraining order, then divorced him. Yet he continued to give support to her and the children. Then, within a year, he discovered that she was sexually active with her psychotherapist. Larry was so fully devastated that he immediately reached out for sympathy, and within three months was married. That marriage may ripen into a healthy bond, but his needs for sympathy and mothering might easily have jeopardized both his judgment and the marriage.

The guidelines for rebonding after the loss of a mature bond are:
1. Wait!
2. Get your grieving done
3. . . . in a non-romantic setting,

4. with trusted, previously established "network" people.
5. Begin slowly with a new bonding,
6. characterized by innocence and
7. slow movement toward intimacy and marriage.

Religious ecstasy. —Again, because intense religious emotion is grounded in the right hemisphere which it shares with all other deep human affections, we are vulnerable to alien bonds when deep religious experience sweeps over us. Charles and Martha Shedd once advised dating couples not to pray together, lest they inadvertently trigger intense sexual feelings. Many campus organizations have a policy that "males will not pray with females," and vice versa, evidently for similar reasons. But a wider caution is needed, since sexual feelings may emerge along same sex lines as easily as in a heterosexual setting. And homosexual link-up with spiritual ecstasy may be at once more confusing to both of the people and also more likely to be consummated sexually, since the taboos are not so well in place to govern sexual contact between males or between females as in the heterosexual situation. The better guideline, I suspect, is that we experience religious ecstasy, intense praying, and celebrating before God always in the larger group setting. Faith is, after all, God's gift to "community" and we are called not to private or exclusivistic cells of belief, but to celebration in community. Elsewhere I have cautioned against intensive "two-couple" friendships. And nowhere are they more vulnerable to sexual confusion than in the intimate spiritual experiences which heighten all affective sensitivities. Again, the healthier settings are those with larger numbers—couples groups of three or more pairs, and singles' groups of ten or twelve are ideal for ski retreats, Bible studies, and prayer cells.

The Schizophrenic Bond

I met Bob, then nineteen, when I joined his family to grieve the loss of their mother. I was the officiating minister. Bob was in university, and his friend Nan had joined the family as Bob's partner. The other siblings were married and some had children. Perhaps because he was still technically living at home, or because he was as yet not engaged or married, I sensed that Bob was harder hit by the loss of the mother.

Then, three months after the funeral, Bob phoned to say he needed some help. He and Nan had had intercourse a couple of times. Both of them repented of it, didn't want it to continue, but he felt helpless. "If I see her, I can just tell we're going to be in bed together again."

The struggle continued into the summer, almost a year after his mother's funeral. And the sexual intimacy was overloading the relationship. Then, after Bob and Nan had shown up in their usual places on Sunday morning, that Sunday evening Bob brought Nell to church. I was a little startled. "Nell and I were in junior college together—before we transferred to different universities."

But I could not have been prepared for the episode which followed. Bob came to me on Tuesday. "I've got an emergency," he said on the phone.

"You met Nell. Well, she wanted to fix supper for me after church. Then she stayed all night. We had intercourse literally all night long. I couldn't believe it. And I don't know what to do. I still love Nan, and I want to marry her in the worst way. In fact, last night I went to see her, and we made love again."

Bob was caught in a schizophrenic bond. On his way toward marriage, his premarital intercourse with Nan seems to have broken his resistance to explicit sexual encounter, and the widely experienced Nell gave him a night he will never forget. Nell, it turns out, is promiscuous. Never mind, Bob bonded to her in that four-year-long acquaintance, during which he admired her, but never dated. Now Nell rang the phone to offer comfort during his grief at the loss of his mother. And the intimate encounter was virtually instant.

Bob's tragedy was explicitly adultery: he bonded to two women. The crime was against Nan, of course, but Bob is likely to suffer longer from the schizophrenic heart. Nell will stalk his memory all his days, but for her it was evidently only "one night of fun." Promiscuous people tend to have lost their bonding ability.

How does one protect against adultery? Bob might have said on the phone, "Let me bring Nan and we will meet you." Or, "No, not tonight, Nan and I have a custom of being in church. Can we meet you tomorrow night somewhere?" My old dictum applies here as well as to the very young:

Absolute privacy
predicts
Absolute intimacy!

And there is nothing to make a statement more clear than the presence of the bonded lover. With today's high freedom and with so many young adults having complete privacy, the tendency is toward both promiscuity and adultery with their tragic long-term consequences.

Early in my teaching experience, I met Peter, a young seminarian. He was engaged to be married in the summer. His fiancée was out of state for college spring break. Peter was in Lexington helping with a youth retreat. He stopped for coffee at Jerry's restaurant. His fiancée's best friend was a waitress there.

"I get off in thirty minutes. Will you wait? Then I won't have to get a cab to go to my apartment." Then as he dropped Maggie off, "Why don't you come up and I'll make a fresh pot of coffee?" She did. But she also came out nude. Peter couldn't handle the situation. Peter joined her in bed. Three months later, Peter married. Two years later the marriage ended. Today, Peter is alone, doubts he will ever marry, and is simply shattered at the core of his being. I have watched him in ministry. He is arbitrary with young love in his church. He is punitive in his premarital interrogation. And his own efforts at dating are seriously flawed by the collapse of his innocence, which is, now fifteen years later, unhealed.

Bob and Peter were vulnerable. They may even have fantasized about the prospect of an "off the record" sexual encounter with Nell and Maggie. I could rehearse other accounts of people who were presented by naked men or naked women and who found a way to bring sobriety back to the moment. I suspect that any of us is capable of adultery, given the right seduction. We somehow do not calculate the emotional cost of such an affair and see only the tantalizing pleasure—heightened because the fruit is stolen.

Jesus knew the tendency toward adultery, so in the famous "Sermon on the Mount" he cautioned that adultery does not begin at dinner before an "all night stand" or at midnight in "absolute privacy with its invitation to absolute intimacy." Not at all: "You have heard, that it was said, 'Do not commit adultery.' But I tell you that anyone who looks at a woman lustfully has already committed adultery with her in his heart" (Matt. 5:27–28). Jesus was scorching men, but a similar caution could be phrased for women, too, since "adultery of the heart" is not the exclusive temptation of men.

Jesus knew what Masters and Johnson think they have discovered in the twentieth century: The largest human sex organ is the brain. That is where the sexual imagination will either construct a virginal vision and muster the energy to live it out in a lifelong exclusive relationship or that same imagination will construct a promiscuous vision of self-gratification pursued at the cost of scrambling one's own bonding capacity and of confusing the affectional systems of the partners.

Adultery (sexual schizophrenia) begins and sets up residence in the mind. "How intimate can we be and not sin?" is a question that always evokes a smile from me. I quote Jesus, then say, "Some people are not safe at a thousand yards. But others will not let anything bad happen to you, even with you snuggling in their arms." The key is "lust."

"Lust" here and elsewhere in the New Testament is not a reference to simple sexual awareness, or to explicit sexual images. It is built on a Greek word which has at its heart the sense of "hot pursuit, capturing and using for one's own purposes." It is a word associated with the idea of "being in heat," or under the spell of involuntary instinctual sexual pursuit. St. Paul widens the use of "lust" when he cautions us to "Flee also youthful lusts," (KJV) or as the New International Version translates it: "Flee the evil desires of youth, and pursue righteousness, faith, love and peace, along with those who call on the Lord out of a pure heart" (2 Tim. 2:22). Sex is not the only thing after which humans "lust." When a young person becomes fixated on an automobile, a career, a prize, or winning a contest, for example, it can be at the level of "lust." "I want it so bad, I don't care if it kills me getting it" is a hyperbolic exaggeration, but it often discloses the essense of lust.

Sexual "lusting" consistently refers to specific fantasies of sexual use of a particular person (a) without concern for the well-being of the person, or the person's active participation in a relationship, and (b) without the prelude of constructing a relationship and consummating the relationship in intimacy within a marriage. But one is not indulging in lust when (a) the sight of a gorgeous human specimen evokes sexual awareness that is nonexploitative, or (b) the vision sees the person united with some appropriate person in an appropriate timeline protected by marriage.

Jesus holds us responsible for what we do in our thoughts. It is not enough that we avoid jumping in and out of other people's beds, we are our brothers' and our sisters' keepers at the level of our imagination. Schizophrenic bonding begins in the mind, and it is the brain that will continue to haunt the memory should "adultery stalk one's very life."

Adultery in History

In the Judeo-Christian tradition adultery was originally punishable by death. Adultery, like murder, was too disruptive of community life, hence was handled radically: it was rooted out by killing both persons involved. It is typical in stone age cultures that the death penalty is invoked to control adultery. And what is also virtually universal is the tendency to regard women as the property of their men. Hence it is the crime against the "owner" that is avenged by the double punishment of his woman and her consort. Carried further, many primitive cultures kill pregnant young women for whom no male will come forward to provide dowry and protection.

So, historically, it has been women who have paid the highest prices for adultery, since they have been regarded as the property of men, and their sexual investment in adultery tends to leave them with longer and more confining obligations. In the text which opens John 8, the story is of a woman "caught in the very act of adultery." Yet there is no man on trial. It is hard to imagine how a woman might be caught in the act without the man also being caught. John 8:1–11, which is not included in most of the old manuscripts, is the only biblical text that seems to be carrying out Leviticus 20:10—"If a man commits adultery with another man's wife—with the wife of his neighbor—both the adulterer and the adulteress must be put to death."

The Ten Commandments simply caution, "You shall not commit adultery" (Deut. 5:18).

But it is Jesus who interferes with the execution of the woman in the John 8 story. The teachers of the law and the Pharisees brought the woman to Jesus, quoted the law demanding her death, then said,

"Now what do you say?"
But Jesus bent down and started to write on the ground with his finger. When they kept on questioning him, he straightened up and said to them,
"If any one of you is without sin, let him be the first to throw a stone at her." Again he stooped down and wrote on the ground.
At this, those who heard began to go away one at a time, the older ones first, until only Jesus was left, with the woman still standing there. Jesus straightened up and asked her,
"Woman, where are they? Has no one condemned you?"
"No one, sir," she said.
"Then neither do I condemn you," Jesus declared.
"Go now and leave your life of sin."

John 8:4–11

In a less explicit case, Jesus sees through the woman who drew water for him at Jacob's well.

"Go call your husband and come back."
"I have no husband," she replied.
"You are right when you say you have no husband. The fact

is you have had five husbands, and the man you now have is not your husband. What you have just said is quite true."

John 4:16–18

What we see is a pivot point historically in the Judeo-Christian view of adultery. And at this pivot, it would appear a new priority comes into place:

1. Restoration, not extermination, is the goal with participants in adultery.
2. Honesty, whether by public exposure or face-to-face exchange, is more important than past failure.
3. Redemption focuses on future faithfulness, not on past unfaithfulness or even present irregularity.

We live, then, in a community of hope. God who has created all things good is now able to make all things new, through Jesus. And the "pivot" point in history sets us all free to work for restoration, honesty, and redemption.

Healing for a Schizophrenic Heart

Confess your divided heart.—If you "go for the jugular vein" of an alien bond, you will simultaneously break with the alien and confess to the original partner.

"I heard your pair bonding tape," Maureen said, calling from North Carolina. "My husband is bonding with another counselor at the Comprehensive Care Clinic where they work. I'm sure of it. It is not genital, but I am sure that they are very far along in the twelve steps."

"Can you discuss it with him?" I asked.

"I don't know. But I love him enough to try."

Then, a week later, her letter arrived. Bill had listened with her to the tape.

"Yes," he said, "I can see what is happening. But I don't want her. I want you."

The letter was the diary of a nightmare. Bill had gotten out of bed at eleven o'clock after discussing the tape. "I'm going over to tell her I am through with this game we're into."

"Bill was still not home at three in the morning. I

panicked and wanted to go looking for him—them. Then, at three-thirty he came in. He was exhausted. He looked like he had been to the morgue. When he climbed into bed, I wanted to cry for myself, but he rolled toward me, embraced me, and said, 'I don't ever want to get emotionally involved with another woman again in all my life. Thank you for reading me and telling me what was happening.' "

Since our sexual identity and our sexual feelings are wired to the very core of personality, they are often hidden from us. We need the "outside" perspective of someone we can trust. The very best "outside perspective" is that of "our other half"—the spouse. But a trusted confidant and friend is a second good choice. It is imperative that the friend not also be in a highly vulnerable position, or the "objectivity" you need will not be there. Pastors, social workers, psychologists, and psychiatrists are trained to be your "outside, objective perspective" people, but even here, *it is critical that you know by their well-established reputations that they themselves are well grounded and are not going to give you a deformed perspective or, themselves, be vulnerable to your schizophrenic bonding problems.* Unfortunately, a practitioner's scandal has rocked the counseling associations, noting that psychologists and psychiatrists are often preying on the problems which clients bring, and are themselves exploiting the client in a confidential, high trust environment. The troublesome pattern of pastoral failure is no doubt often related to counselor-client alien bonding.

Sexual problems are virtually never solved or the damage healed until there is a confidential "moment of truth" when a trusted and respected confidant hears you out and carries off the weight of your grief. Choosing the confidential person, if you must go beyond the marital partner, is the most difficult of all decisions. But trust your intuition. You will almost always be right if you read faces. You will likely be choosing only people who, themselves, have been through virtually the same "fires" that have almost destroyed you.

Burn the bridge to alien love.—If your primary bond is tethered to *agape* love, then coming home to your original lover and your faithful marriage will become simply a tough matter of "choice."

"I'm going to bite the bullet," Al said to me, "and I have already told Jill it is over. I will never see her again."

We can feel guilt for breaking *eros, philia,* or *storge.* But it is the power of *agape's* choice that will pull us out of the fires of new and alien love.

Jesus told how radical the cure must be to break the adulterous mind:

> If your right eye causes you to sin, gouge it out and throw it away. It is better for you to lose one part of your body than for your whole body to be thrown into hell. And if your right hand causes you to sin, cut it off and throw it away. It is better for you to lose one part of your body than for your whole body to go into hell.
>
> Matthew 5:29–30

These are radical cures. But schizophrenic bonding, adultery, is a profoundly deep fault line at the core of personality. Here is a ripping up of the "bonding steps" that have been inappropriately laid down: eye to body, eye to eye, hand to hand, arm to shoulder, hand to waist, eventually perhaps even hand to genital. Jesus lays the axe at the heart of the bonding trajectory and says, "End it violently, if you must, but end it now. Adultery guarantees you your own private hell. A mutilated body would spell relief by comparison to the living hell of a schizophrenic bond."

Return to the bonded lover. —Maureen's letter describing Bill's return at three-thirty in the morning is the story of prodigal love "coming home, at last." Remember that "repentance" is a word which means "coming home to the truth." But returning to the lover is even more than that. It is coming home to affection, it is beginning to repair again the damaged and typically neglected bond between the pair. But more than that it is coming back to wholeness, to the unity of "two becoming one," to the psychological soundness by which the core of personality is "at peace." If "the adulteress/adulterer stalks your very life," then it is even more true that "the exclusive, lifelong lover breathes life into you, even to old age."

In this chapter, I have wanted you to sense the enormous tragedy of adultery, but also the grand peace that comes with the restoration of the original but damaged bond. In the history of the human race, the good news that any of us who has suffered can be made new again is relatively new news. Nobody needs to be executed as hopeless. We stand just under two thousand years from the "pivot point" when Jesus interrupted an execution to announce that God can make damaged people whole.

QUESTIONS PEOPLE ASK

Q: You seem to suggest that adultery should not necessarily break a marriage. That goes so against everything I have thought that I have trouble with it. My mother divorced my father because he was having an affair, so my dad married the other woman, and I have always felt that my mom did the right thing. Am I wrong?

A: Nobody can make that judgment for someone else, I think. What worries me is that we have created an environment in which our instant "reflexes" have been supported by what we said was a "biblical view of divorce." I simply want to take that support away and to ask whether we dare be "Christian" in our view of moral failure of any kind. "Self-justifying" behavior of any sort is sub-Christian, and our traditional view of "the innocent party" divorcing the "guilty party" has generally been the foundation for the advice we have given which has often dissolved marriages which had a great deal of life left in them. The mature, not to mention Christian perspective always works toward reconciliation, healing, mutual respect, and the restoration of all people. So, we shouldn't be surprised that Jesus would not touch the divorce question to condone it. "Destructive" behavior is distinctly what Jesus is not about. Another "force" feeds self-pity, censure, alienation, and distantiation.

Q: If adultery called for the "death penalty" in the Old Testament and in many stone age cultures, then why isn't it reasonable to at least call it "grounds for divorce" today?

A: Among the secular and pagan peoples of the world, divorce is surely more humane than execution. Among Christians it would seem reasonable to search the behavior and the teachings of Jesus and of the New Testament for a pattern and a word on how to deal with adultery. The fact is, Jesus does not ignore adultery and he does not, as we often do, confuse it with fornication/promiscuity, as I have tried to illustrate throughout this book. If we would be truly Christian we may have to ask how we will deal with divorced people, adulterous people, and "living togethers" with their extralegal arrangements. On all of these we have specific Scripture episodes which show Jesus dealing with just such people. St. Paul also describes the early Christians with the phrase, "such also were some of you." I suspect that many warm-hearted Christians are reflexively reverting to pagan and secular attitudes and judgments when they viciously attack the divorced and divorcing and irregularly bonding people around them.

7

They Made It Home!

△

The best news of all is that many people who have been broken are now mended, and "the grace of God is the glue." They have found that it is true, after all:

God who has created all things good
Can make all things new—through Jesus.

You may find your very own story here. Each of these is "true" in the sense that it really happened. None of the names are "true," because the reconstructed people deserve anonymity. Only they may decide when or whether to tell their story in "first person." But each of them has read the story before it appeared here, and was enthusiastic that his or her tragedy might be turned into even more gracious hope for other people.

Tanya, Paralyzed by Incest—Crying for Outside Help!

Tanya would stop by my office, often playing off some small piece of "business." I was her official academic advisor. Then she made an intentional appointment.

"See, I've got this problem. I just know Robert is going

to ask me to marry him. And I wish I could, but when I think about it I just go to pieces."

She began to cry softly. And she couldn't go on at all.

Three times she made appointments and the conversations were almost exactly the same each time. I was unable to set her free to say what was behind her paralysis. The third time when the tears appeared I responded.

"You know Robbie. I want you to come to the house some evening soon when we are both home, and the three of us will talk." I got my calendar, and together we agreed on an evening just a couple of days away.

I had made a judgment while listening. It ran like this. The issue is sexual. It is taking enormous courage for Tanya to even try to open up some dark page out of her memory. She deserves the strongest possible support for lifting out her "pearl" formed in some past trauma.

In our living room, Tanya began again. The tears interrupted her. But she got further. She was afraid of men, she said, because of something that happened when she was a girl. It was clear that she was stuck. She could not go on.

"Let me finish the story," I said after a long and painful silence. "Your daddy seduced you. How old were you when it happened?"

"Twelve."

"How long did it go on?"

"It never happened again. I refused to be in the house alone with my father—not ever again."

"Did your mother know?"

"No."

"Are you still afraid of him?"

"I still won't be alone with him."

The wound was open. The tragic story was known. With Tanya that seemed to be enough. We held her hands while Robbie and I prayed to invoke God's healing grace. Robert was not a dangerous man. We established that in a light survey of their developing relationship. The monster was the phantom of her father who haunted every male who came into Tanya's world. That night the monster died.

"How do you think this has affected your father?" I asked.

"I don't know."

"Let me predict something. The day will come when you will be able to say to your father, 'Daddy, I have worried about you ever since that day when I was twelve. Are you all right now?' "

"Oh, I could never do that."

"It's OK, but can you imagine how much shame and guilt he has carried for more than ten years?"

Robbie and I watched Tanya over the next couple of years. To our complete surprise, she began to change. Her appearance and her body weight were changing. Then she was engaged, married, and off into ministry.

Four years later the letter came:

"You said it would happen, but I couldn't imagine it would ever be possible. And when I asked Daddy whether he was all right after what had happened then, he burst into tears. He hugged me and told me how he had worried that he had spoiled everything for me. I feel like I got my Daddy back last week when we cried together."

Tanya seemed to know instinctually that so long as she bottled up her memory from age twelve, she would never be able to let it go. For two decades I had been suggesting to students and counselees that they needed to find some trusted person with whom to share past traumatic sexual experiences. "Since these were 'social' events, they require a 'social' healing. That is, you are unlikely to get the healing you need in a solitary prayer vigil with God. It will take a tangible human being to set you free from your guilt."

By the time I was visiting with Tanya in my office, I was wiser. It is shame itself which must be "aired" before other people, I think. Shame, by definition, is a sheath in which we hide ourselves and our feelings of humiliation, inadequacy, and low self-esteem. Shame leads to feelings of such unworthiness that one uses violent images to contemplate the future: "I am a slut, a whore, a sex maniac, a 'crazy,' and the world would be better off without me." But shame, when owned and exposed, may be transformed either into guilt or into absolution. In Tanya's case, she needed to watch our faces, see our acceptance, and know that she was not responsible for what had happened long ago. And with our judgment pronounced in the form of complete affirmation, Tanya was free at last.

In other cases, the transformation of shame into guilt is a grand leap toward forgiveness. It allows the guilty person to say, "I am responsible; I have sinned; I must pay." And the listener is then enabled by Jesus to say, "On the authority of the words of Jesus in John chapter 20 I want you to know that your sins are forgiven. Leave them here." And the listener becomes the agent of God's forgiving grace.

In our exploration of how people "come home," let Tanya represent those who follow the path of crying for "outside help"!

Jim, Who Didn't Know—Telling the Truth!

His first intercourse came when he was fourteen, and it continued through college, always casual. Jim never thought of himself as promiscuous, just "normal." In fact, he was in Sunday school and church every week. His family was prominent and respected in the community. Then when Jim was twenty-two, after God got hold of his life, he realized that he had damaged a lot of people and that the woman he now wanted to date was another in that series he had met who came to him with complete innocence. The engagement was just around the corner when Jim unpacked his story and cried out for help.

Then came the moment of truth in the relationship with Mary. This innocent, virginal beauty asked him about his own innocence. And as a man of integrity he fumbled but found words to tell the truth. She was devastated. It was an evening of tears and sobbing for both of them.

"I didn't know what I had been playing with," Jim told me. "And there is no way I can get it back—my innocence."

Across half a year I had occasional conversations with both Jim and Mary. While the remorse and despairing over something lost forever was a plague on Jim, the plague of superiority was nibbling away just as certainly at Mary.

"How could he have done that? Why didn't he think of us? Is he just a breeding animal? Will he do this for the rest of his life?" The accusations and assaults billowed out.

"Why do you think Jim told you all of this?" I asked her one day.

"Because I asked him, I suppose."

"But most people would have lied and would have told you what you wanted to hear. Why do you think Jim told you the whole truth, even though it reduced him to sobbing hours of humiliation and pain?"

"Because he loves me and has to be truthful with me?"

"If you have found a truthful man," I went on, "you have found a whole man. Whatever he may have been through, he is pure and safe. If I were predicting, I would hazard a guess that you are less likely to have to deal with adultery in your marriage than many women whose husbands appear to be innocent, but have never found their way to the truth foundation in their marriages."

So, a few months later, there we all stood. They were both dressed in white, and people in their community still comment on how meaningful were the vows they wrote and exchanged. "What depth! I don't think I ever heard a couple speak to each other in the wedding with such sincerity!"

Welcome home, Jim. "Repentance" has a profound and deep meaning we seldom contemplate: "coming home to the truth." We cannot repent when we are trapped in the sheath of shame, because shame is preoccupied with narcissistic protection. If there is an obvious and public pregnancy, then it blushes, wants to hide, to deny, or to run away. There is no repentance that ever arises from shame. There may be tears, even prayers for forgiveness, even sobbing on the shoulder of parents, friends, or lovers. But the language and motive are consistently protecting the self. "I feel so ashamed! I am so embarrassed!" one young man said as he paced the floor of our home. He was trying to figure out what to do about the pregnancy he was responsible for "back home" and that was threatening to explode in his present college campus world. His solution, finally— a secret abortion at his expense—gave him some relief, but he never came home to the truth. Integrity never won out at the core of his being. So repentance has not yet become an option for him.

Jim, on the other hand, was eager to retrace his steps in adolescent promiscuity, to expose it to a trusted confidant, and then to own the reality of his own past irresponsibility as he embraced a woman who was being wounded all those years, and who now could confirm his forgiveness.

Bobby, a Ticket to Fly—Breaking with Idols!

When Bobby was fifteen, barely into dating, his father stopped him in the driveway.

"Here, take these. If you're going to be dating, I expect you to take every pretty girl to bed, or you are no son of mine."

"But. . . ."

"Go on. I'm serious."

Bobby locked the condoms in the glove compartment of his car.

"I had not, at that time, even thought of having sex with the girl I was dating. I liked her. I thought she was cool. And I wanted to be near her and to take her to school events where we could be seen together. Now, I was confronted with a whole new set of feelings. I can see now that my father actually seduced me with those words and that box of condoms."

Bobby told how his father's words ate on him. "You're no son of mine. . . ." And the father's suggested agenda became a priority.

"I had sex with the three girls I dated between age fifteen and the time I left for state university and my football scholarship. But I felt enormous guilt. My mother and I went to church almost every week, and I felt like something in me had died. At the university, though, I met some Campus Crusade guys who were so free and spontaneous that they reminded me of how happy I had been as a boy, and before Thanksgiving I was saved. I was absorbed immediately in the Bible studies. I didn't date for nearly two years. By then I knew I was free again, and I had already decided that Lou Ann was the woman I was going to marry."

Within a year of Bobby's first intercourse at his father's coaching, his parents were divorced. Bobby's father had been promiscuous in the mid-life fling that too often occurs when faith and fidelity have not been forged into a peaceful marriage. And like King David's adultery, Bobby's father's promiscuity contaminated the innocence of the next generation. "Mid-life crisis" and "adolescent crisis" often form two parallel layers in the home, and the teens are highly susceptible to adult failure, but rarely are the parents so directly seductive as was Bobby's father.

Today Bobby and Lou Ann are into the second decade of their virginal marriage, lovers of the first order. The breach between Bobby and his father is not healing well. But last year there was a gesture toward some reconciliation.

"I phoned to borrow Dad's twelve-gauge shotgun," Bobby told me. "Dad brought it by and left it, and with it a letter. The letter told how his father had once owned the gun, and that one day it would be mine. But for now, it is on loan only during pheasant season."

Bobby was seduced by the most powerful of social pressures: his own father's infidelity which was made explicit in the tangible seduction of advice and equipment to fly away into promiscuity. More often, it is peer influence which gives the explicit push into early sexual experimentation. But all of the studies in sexual behavior point to the relative safety of a stable family structure in which both father and mother are active in parent care. Boys in such homes are far less likely than boys without fathers to be sexually active in high school. So Bobby was particularly vulnerable. He thought of his father as a man of integrity, yet his father specifically demanded that he enter the world of sexual activity.

Fortunately, every teen eventually yearns to establish an identity separate from the parental nest. And for Bobby, the entry into university allowed him to rediscover his virginal dream. Some hunger for innocence and integrity was keeping Bobby unsettled and hungry to return to the dream of his boyhood. Perhaps that hunger is universal. But many people lose touch with it. Most addictions revolve around efforts to block out memory and the impossible dream of lifelong innocence. "There is a light that lights every person that comes into the world," is the way the Gospel writer describes the hunger in John chapter one. And John Wesley in another century talked about "preventing grace." By such grace, Wesley wanted to describe how God both plants a hunger in every human—which cannot be satisfied short of intimate relationship with God—with the accompanying holiness and love which come from such a holy relationship. But Wesley also used the term to describe how God uses this inner yearning to "prevent" the person from simply wandering on through life from one misadventure to another in a descending spiral of quick self-destruction. So Bobby can look back and rejoice that his heart was kept tender toward honesty and integrity and that he did not move quickly into an irreversible, promiscuous path.

Darlene, Who Loved Too Much—Redefining Love's Boundaries!

"We took this high school boy whose parents were divorcing. Jack and I both felt sorry for him, and Jack suggested that we let him finish his senior year in the same school—by living with us."

Darlene described the arrangement. Childless in the eighth year of their marriage, and looking age thirty in the face, they were ready for a "child" of almost any age. So Ralph seemed like one answer to that yearning for a child.

"I don't know what did it exactly. At first I could just think of him as a guest in the house. But then, doing laundry, sitting at the table several times a week with him, sometimes just the two of us when Jack was out of town—something did it. I had hugged him as I would my own child, from the day we first discussed inviting him into the house. But suddenly I knew I was not just loving him as a mother would. I was in love with him in a very sexual way."

The adulterous bond was consummated before Ralph's graduation in the spring. Jack knew that his marriage had been upstaged by Darlene's new devotion to caring for Ralph. But it was more than a year after Ralph had left the house that Jack confronted Darlene and demanded to know whether "anything had gone on between her and Ralph."

"I was aching to go to Ralph, to visit him at college, and
to sleep with him. I couldn't lie to Jack, not so much because
I was such an honest person. I was vulnerable because I
was hurting so bad. And I was losing my feelings for Jack.
God knows they had been in bad shape even before Ralph
moved in."

Now it was Jack's turn. The first years were characterized
by gestures of superiority, almost of blackmail—small
threats to expose Darlene to her family if she made any
complaints against his schedule away from home or of his
lack of sexual interest in her. Eight years after Darlene's
adulterous affair with Ralph, Jack openly flaunted a "girl
friend" to Darlene, tantalizing her with secrecy, implying
that "everything is platonic, not sexual," but spending more
and more time away.

Now Darlene faces the prospect of being alone at mid-
life, still childless. Her journeys to integrity came at a high
price, but she has God's peace, a sense of direction and
vocation, and could visit with you about possible meanings
of "celibacy" as a Christian way for people who are recover-
ing from misadventures in intimacy.

Today Darlene struggles with her failure. "I wonder
whether I am safe around young men in any setting," she
says. "Yet I know that they are safe around me. I see now
that I confused my maternal love and sexual love. Today
I know that I cancelled my 'mother' love for Ralph when
I engaged him in sexual love. The two are mutually exclusive. So I teach and work in the church around young men
with a sense of freedom now, because I truly love them,
and that closes the door on any kind of sexual intimacy.
They will be special to someone, but it will not be me."

Sexual desire may be triggered in almost any environment, if the pair bonding exchanges are available—the eye,
voice, and touch opportunities. But it is best prevented
when we keep a clear boundary between *storge* parental
concern and *eros* adoration.

Paul, Everybody Needs Love—Retargeting Eros!

Paul was an only child. I met him when he was a middler
in seminary. He phoned me at about midnight.

"You don't know me," he began, "but I know you, and I think I can trust you." I heard a train in the background, and knew that in our small village he was calling from a phone booth some distance from the campus.

"My mother caught me with my best friend," he said, "and she really blew a gasket. She told me I would grow up to be a homosexual, and I guess she was right."

Paul told how that incident when he was six years old, playing doctor with a next-door neighbor boy, was indelibly etched in his brain. He had done occasional mutual masburbation when he had an "overnight" with a cousin or other close male friend.

"It was strange, looking back on it. We did it because it felt good, but something else happened. Those guys were special friends. They still are. I have a different feeling for them. Nobody ever knew what we had done, but we knew, and it formed a kind of secret attachment between us. In fact, I think I came to respect every other male I ever met. I respected them a little more, because I knew what males were about, how complicated they were, and I knew what deep feelings of attachment went with their sexual activity—if they had any.

"I was loved," he said, "at a very important time in my life, in a home with two busy parents and no brothers and sisters. And not one of the dozen or so guys I was intimate with ever thought of being 'homosexual' or 'gay.' Instead, we knew that we were rehearsing for marriage, and we often talked about how good that would be."

By the time Paul went to college, he said, it had been several years since he had had genital contact with any of the boys out of his childhood. But the first semester on campus, one of the track scholarship men invited him to pace him on nightly runs. There was an overt sexual advance, and another set of feelings awakened in Paul.

"I looked in the phone book and found a hotline for sexual problems. I felt safe with that. It was a city of a million people, so I unloaded on the woman who answered. She said I would receive a call right back. It was a minister. He said he would pick me up in front of the library on our campus in a half hour. Instead of helping me sort things out, he took me to bed."

When I met Paul it had been five years since the minister's night and the homosexual label and lifestyle had enclosed Paul. When he returned to campus the next day, he began a four-year trek of "giving up" on getting a single mind on his sexual identity. He began finding one-night stands with strangers, at first developing short-term friendships with them, but eventually using a pseudonym for himself and suggesting the same practice by his partners. "I didn't really want to know who they were. I didn't want to have to deal with them as people."

Paul had abandoned the promiscuous pattern before seminary. His call to me was a cry for help when the impulse to return to promiscuity had hit him. I helped get him into immediate therapy, and the progress was steady, but not spectacular. Today, he has married, but with children now in the home, the ghosts of his confused sexual identity still haunt him. He is in sex orientation therapy, and is making progress toward eliminating the tattoo images that threaten to divide his life and destroy his marriage.

Paul is coming home. The path back from promiscuity of any sort is often long, painful, and subject to occasional detours. "Keep the pattern of the last ten years in perspective," I suggested once to Paul. Just as sexual appetite is "orientation," so also is repentance and obedience. "Let's celebrate the fact that . . ." and we reflected for a few minutes on life patterns of shame, deception, seduction, anonymity, and sexual addiction that have been long gone out of his behavior.

Integrity is a choice, just as *agape* is a choice. *Agape* chooses not only whom to love, but sometimes is able to choose which sexual preference one will cultivate and which one will allow God's healing grace to extinguish.

Epilogue: Some Tips for Coming Home!

The stories here are but a small sample of the millions that could be told. Each story is different in detail, but many parallel the major lines of these living parables. And many stories do not move in such positive directions. If you are one of those who feels that life as you have known it on this planet has ended, then check off this list to see whether you have deliberately given yourself a chance to let Jesus make you new again:

1. *Outside help?* Is there one person to whom you could unload the detail of your shame and guilt, and accept their offer to "carry half of your load" or their pronouncement of sins forgiven, based on John 20 and Jesus' command to Spirit-filled people?

2. *The whole truth?* Have you given the whole truth to anyone? Or are you protecting "narcissistic" interests, wanting to "look good"? Try writing out in a secret journal the complete detail of your failure. Tell it all. Lock the journal up! Then ask yourself whether there is some trusted person to whom you could either give the journal or give an oral version of the full story? Repentance and forgiveness require going to the bottom of the whole story and owning responsibility for it all, including responsibility for making responsible present choices about reconciliation and restitution.

3. *Breaking idolatries?* Can you name the idols whose service requires you to continue in your promiscuity, infidelity, or other destructive pattern? Are they respected friends, relatives, colleagues? Are they business or pleasure partners? Are you caught in the service of a pornographic media and music idolatry? Are you deadening your spiritual sensitivity with addictive patterns involving food, drink, or other chemicals? Is the "God-shaped vacuum" in your heart being stuffed with things which never satisfy its appetite, but only deaden the sensitivity to holiness and love? If so, make a choice. Make a small choice, perhaps. But begin your journey home. And it begins with one step. Phone somebody now and tell that trusted friend you are coming home.

4. *Learning to love?* Love can be a very confusing package. You are not the only person who has confused affection with sexual awakening. Join the club. Now are you going to stay confused? Or will you let Jesus help you sort out your many-splendored loves and intentionally target them into appropriate relationships? Can you trust someone with the story of your own misadventures? If so, the forgiving covenant will come to you, and you will be blessed by having

a confidant to whom to be lightly accountable, but you will also have a friend who will bolster your loving heart and liberate it to love again—in all of the right ways available to *philia, storge,* and *agape.*

5. *Confused orientation?* So you have made the gestures of sexual love not only at the wrong time, but with the wrong sex? If you are a male, the probabilities of that happening when you are young are quite high. The external genitalia and the erection system make boys vulnerable to same-sex activity. But the male brain is formed from the female brain format during the sixteenth to the twenty-sixth weeks of a pregnancy. And not all male brains form in the same degree of "masculinity." So part of male sexual response has to be learned—from family observation, and by personal choice. The largest study of male sexual behavior found that nearly forty percent of all males experience some mixed orientation and preference. So, come on home. Just as *agape* is a choice, so also is sexual preference. Find a nicely married couple whom you can trust. Remember Jesus' caution not to cast your pearls before swine! But when you know you are safe, tell the whole truth. Tell them you are ready to come home. And welcome. You will be there!

Notes

1. The Mystery of Human Bonding

1. See Daniel Levinson, et al., *The Seasons of a Man's Life* (New York: Ballantine Books, 1978).

2. Sophocles, David Green, tr., *Philoctetes*. See lines 650–660; lines 670–678 discuss *phileo*.

3. See Jose Ortega y Gasset, tr. Toby Talbot, *On Love* (New York: Meridian Books, 1957) p. 31.

4. See my *Bonding: Relationships in the Image of God*, chapter 3, "Pair Bonding: What God Joins Together" (Waco: Word, Inc., 1985). See also Desmond Morris, *Intimate Behavior* (New York: Random House, 1971). I have adapted and abbreviated his names for the twelve steps of "pair bonding," observed universally among humans.

5. C. S. Lewis, *The Four Loves* (New York: Harcourt, Brace & World, Inc., 1960). Here Lewis devotes an entire book to unfolding implications of the four facets of love in one of the most refreshing and truly affectional books in the English language.

6. Sheldon Vanauken, *A Severe Mercy* (New York: Harper and Row, 1971).

7. *A Severe Mercy*, p. 176. Used by permission.

2. Naked and Unashamed: The Universal Human Yearning

1. I tried for most of my life to ignore Jesus' clear words about "forgiving sins." But it was Mildred Wynkoop on our campus several years ago who cautioned that we must take John 20:19–23 as a unit. "We cannot have it both ways—taking our favorite parts out of the teaching." It either all hangs together, or we must not claim it for ourselves: "As the Father has sent me, I am sending you." And with that he breathed on them and said, "Receive the Holy Spirit. If you forgive anyone his

sins, they are forgiven; if you do not forgive them, they are not forgiven."
If you wish to explore it further with me, send $5 and a return envelope
to SPO 944, Wilmore, Kentucky 40390, requesting the tape, "Let Jesus
Breathe on You!" It is an expository sermon which unfolds the teaching here, with implications for all believers—not just for ordained
clergy!

2. Here I have used "human" for the ambiguous "Adam" so as not
to confuse the image of God which consists of both male and female,
as indicated in Genesis 1:26–28. I have also repeated the name of Deity
so as not to suggest the distortion with which I grew up, namely the
idea that a male God created a male human, and afterward as something
of an afterthought created a female, largely for the benefit of the man.
The Genesis 2 account suggests instead that full humanity was in Adam,
that the differentiation of the human into male and female was accom-
plished by a surgical separation, and there the name Adam used for
the united male and female gives way to "Issha" for the woman who
is created sexually differentiated before "Ish" awakens and cries out
for her. See my treatment in "On Splitting the Adam!" in *Bonding:
Relationships in the Image of God,* chapter 2 (Waco: Word, Inc., 1985).

3. For the entire text of the Broadway musical, see *Hair,* edited by
the staff of Fotonovel Publications, Los Angeles, 1979.

4. Read the Noah embarrassment story in Genesis 9:18–28.

5. Deuteronomy 24:1–4. See also footnote 1 for chapter four.

6. Matthew 19:9. The New International Version translates fornication
as "marital unfaithfulness" and is distinctly unhelpful both in our understanding about divorce in general and the tragedy of fornication, promiscuity, and sexual addiction, in particular. See my chapters 4 and 5 here
for a distinction that will help you unscramble things you may have
observed and worried about for some time.

7. See the Jacob-Rachel-Leah-Jacob story in Genesis 29.

8. See the entire advice in 1 Corinthians 7, but note this cryptic, "bot-
tom-line" advice in 7:9.

9. See my "Life as Pilgrimage," in *Moral Development Foundations:
Judeo-Christian Alternatives to Piaget/Kohlberg* (Nashville: Abingdon,
1983). See especially pages 13 ff. If you have further interest in following
implications of this developmental trajectory from shame to guilt, you
may wish to look at the following: "Some Critical Adaptations for Judaeo-
Christian Communities," my contribution to Sohan and Celia Modgil,
Lawrence Kohlberg: Consensus and Controversy (Sussex, U. K.: Falmer
Press, 1985). "The Contemporary Church as 'Holy Community': Call
to Corporate Character and Life," my chapter in Melvin E. Dieter and
Daniel N. Berg, *The Church: An Inquiry into Ecclesiology from a Biblical
Theological Perspective* (Anderson: Warner Press, Inc., 1984). "Pain: Ca-
talayst for Christian Holiness," my contribution to *Preacher's Magazine,*
Volume 58, Number 4 (Beacon Hill Press, Kansas City, June, 1983). "Some
Biblical Foundations and Metaphors of Vocational Ideals in the Wesleyan
Tradition," in the papers from a conference at Emory University, edited

by Theodore Runyan, *Wesleyan Theology Today: A Bicentennial Theological Consultation* (Nashville: United Methodist Publishing House, 1985).

3. Tragedy Comes in Two Colors: Promiscuity and Double Bonding

1. Read 1 Corinthians 7:3–4 in several translations. Notice that the men are challenged first!

2. Ann Landers told the boy's story in her column released on 9 June 1985. In it she also urged everyone to put parents and children in touch with METRO HELP. Headquarters are at 2210 North Halsted in Chicago. Their nationwide toll-free number is 1-800-621-4000 and is open every day at all hours. She further recommended, and I applaud the choice, Father Bruce Ritter's Covenant House in New York City, at 1-212-354-4323. Ms. Landers also publicized the fact that Trailways Bus began, in 1984, a program they call "Home Free." They work with police, verifying with the parents, and a ticket is provided to put the young person on board without arrest, fine, or further interrogation.

3. Examine the evidence that soft porn is really "anti-relational sex," see Gay Talese, *Thy Neighbor's Wife* (Garden City: Doubleday, 1981). He reports on the history of the launching of *Playboy* in a two-chapter biography of Hugh Hefner. A most revealing picture inside the *Playboy* mansion appears in Peter Bogdanovich, *The Killing of the Unicorn: Dorothy Stratten, 1960–1980* (New York: William Morrow and Company, 1984). In this tribute to the murdered *Playboy* Playmate of the Year in 1980, Peter Bogdanovich makes his own confession and is generous in confessing for Hugh Hefner, too. Their lifestyle led to her murder, Bogdanovich concludes. The sadistic and demonic orgies that destroy thousands of women for the violent satisfaction of deformed men unfold here in amazing and tragic repentance.

4. See Daniel Levinson, et al., *The Seasons of a Man's Life* (New York: Ballantine Books, 1978).

5. 1 Corinthians 6:9–11 where, following a list of all sorts of tragic patterns of sexual behavior, including promiscuity/fornication, St. Paul says, "And that is what some of you were. But you were washed, you were sanctified, you were justified in the name of the Lord Jesus Christ and by the Spirit of our God."

4. Grounds for Divorce?

1. The actual meaning of "nakedness" or "indecency" is not at all clear. Two of my students in the spring of 1985, Gary Carr and Richard Bennett, helped me by devoting considerable research to this and other "word studies" related to sexual matters in the Old Testament and the

New Testament. The Hebrew nouns *ervat davar* are placed end to end
for this unusual word. They are literally "naked thing/word." The same
pair of words appears in Deuteronomy 23:14, there referring to God's
discovery of a "hidden thing" in Israel which warranted God's rejecting
Israel. There is no explicit sexual behavior indicated by the two nouns,
but then there is no explicit sexual content when we say "he took her
to bed." We have perhaps forever lost the actual cultural connotation
from the time the phrase was used. It was hotly contested by the two
popular rabbinic schools: Hillel taught that it simply referred to any
trivial displeasure a woman brought to a man. Shammai laminated sexual
disgrace with it. If Jesus is, indeed, alluding to the Jewish taboo in Deuteronomy 24:1–4 with his "fornication" statement, he must have thought
of it in sexual terms much as I have expressed it here.

2. See William H. Masters and Virginia E. Johnson, *The Pleasure
Bond*, chapter 7, "Swinging Sex: Is There a Price to Pay?" (New York:
Bantam Books, 1976) pp. 148–185.

3. *The Pleasure Bond*, chapter 8, "What Sexual Fidelity Means in a
Marriage," pp. 186–203. The citation is from pp. 201–202.

4. See my chapter, "Pair Bonding: What God Joins Together," in
Bonding: Relationships in the Image of God, or chapter 1 here, "The
Mystery of Human Bonding."

5. *Bonding: Relationships in the Image of God*, see especially chapter
4, "What Has Gone Wrong with the Bonding?"

6. Isabel Briggs Myers, *Introduction to Type*, and her *Gifts Differing*
(Consulting Psychologists Press, 577 College Avenue, Palo Alto, CA
94306, 1976 and 1980). The Briggs Myers personality inventory is a "de-
scriptive" test, not a diagnostic test. As such it identifies preferences
and the "gift package" of the individual in nonevaluative ways and serves
to enhance self-esteem and to enlarge the vision of valuing the diversity
which is everywhere in the Creation—especially in human personality
differences.

7. *Bonding: Relationships in the Image of God*, see "Pair Bonding:
What God Joins Together."

8. For an example of Jesus in action, notice his behavior and judgment
shown regarding divorced and sexually damaged persons in Luke 7, John
4, and John 8. These are commonly ignored by people who set about
to tell us "what the Bible teaches about divorce and sexual failure."

9. See "Who Is Holding Your Trampoline?" in *Bonding: Relationships
in the Image of God*.

10. For a thorough analysis-outline of the full gamut of Old and New
Testament teachings on divorce, remarriage, and all related issues in
this chapter, including the conclusions about God's grace and the "new
creation" of one's past, see Wilber T. Dayton, Wayne E. Caldwell, and
Carl Schultz, *Marriage: The Biblical Perspective* (Marion: The Wesley
Press, 1984).

11. See "What Has Gone Wrong with the Bonding?" in *Bonding: Relationships in the Image of God*.

5. Is There Life after Promiscuity?

1. When *porneia* comes into English it takes both the fornication and the pornography forms. This split from "porn" to "forn" and back again to "porn" is explained by the famous Grimm's Law of linguistics. You can trace Grimm's Law in any basic book dealing with the history of the English language.

2. Sexual Addiction Counseling, largely shaped by Patrick Carnes's work, reported in his book *Out of the Shadows: Understanding Sexual Addiction*, (CompCare Publications, 2415 Annapolis Lane, Minneapolis, MN 55441) may be contacted at a toll-free number, 1-800-328-5099. You may request information about workshops, as well as a brochure about sexual addiction. Dr. Carnes's offices are at Human Development Center, 1925 Nicollet Avenue, Minneapolis, MN 55403, phone 612-871-7388. Sex Addicts Anonymous (S.A.A.) may be contacted at P.O. Box 1532, Northbrook, IL 60062. A similar group calling itself Sexaholics Anonymous (SA) may be reached at The New York Founders Group of SA, P.O. Box 1542, New York, NY 10185, phone: 212-570-7292, or on the West Coast at Sexaholics Anonymous, P.O. Box 300, Simi Valley, CA 93062.

3. Marguerite R. and Marshall L. Shearer, *Adolescent Sexuality*, in *Audio Digest, Pediatrics*, Volume 21, Number 10, 27 May 1975, 1250 South Glendale Avenue, Glendale, CA 91205.

4. See, for example, E. Mavis Hetherington and Jan L. Deur, "The Effects of Father Absence on Child Development," *Young Children*, 36, (March 1971) pp. 233–242.

5. See "The sex systems," in my *Bonding: Relationships in the Image of God*, pp. 160 ff.

6. As a single example of how easily the myth of the sex magazines explodes, read Stephen Board's assault on the soft porn hucksters in his "The Joy of Chastity: His Contemplating the Bust of Hugh Hefner," in *HIS*, February, 1975, p. 1. Then compare the best research statistics in the U.S.A. and in France where these trends are visible. Using the famous Kinsey studies as a base, France is in decline on frequencies of intercourse across the last twenty-five years, falling one per week. U.S.A. averages are down since Kinsey by about 1.5 per week, the only exception being the "religious women" in the *Redbook* study, who turn out to be most active. Their frequencies are up from the Kinsey frequency measures. One might conclude that the so-called "sexual revolution" has diminished actual sexual intimacy for the general population, but that those who are alive to God have found new freedom in sexual expressions—consistently in exclusive, marital relationships.

7. See "The sex systems," cited above.

8. See David Elkind, "Teenagers in Crisis," in *All Grown Up and No Place to Go* (Menlo Park: Addison-Wesley, 1984).

9. See, for example, "Why Religious Women Are Good Lovers," in *Redbook* magazine, April, 1976, pp. 103 f f.

10. Phyllis Trible, "An Unnamed Woman: The Extravagance of Violence," in *Texts of Terror* (Philadelphia: Fortress Press, 1984). See also, for positive perspectives on the feminine and female characteristics of the divine, *God and the Rhetoric of Sexuality.*

11. The UPI press release article I read in the *Chicago Tribune,* during the week of 20 March 1985, entitled "Hefner suffers stroke, opts for new philosophy." See also Gay Talese, *Thy Neighbor's Wife.* Two chapters are devoted to a biography of Hugh Hefner, with a chronicle of his descent into pornography and into his own personal promiscuity, with the disintegrating side effects it brought by mid-life.

12. See Dick Polman's "Centerfold being shifted at *Playboy,*" *Chicago Tribune,* Section D, Tuesday, May 7, 1985.

13. See William Glasser, *Reality Therapy* (New York: Harper and Row, 1965). See also his *Stations of the Mind* (Harper and Row, 1981).

14. Margie Lewis, *The Hurting Parent* (Grand Rapids: Zondervan, 1980).

15. It is interesting to speculate on what the blasphemy was which removed Hymenaeus and Alexander from the Christian community. It may have been some resistance to God-ordained authority, but it is possible that it could have been a problem of sexual behavior. Homosexuality is at its root a blasphemy against the divine image in which we are created: male and female, such that "calling evil good" or "calling good evil" may include "calling the part the whole," or "calling the whole part" would constitute the ultimate blasphemy against the nature of the divine Person. Hence "the broken image" or "symbolic confusion" are terms which express a tragedy deeper than mere violations of protocol or social convention: they may denote blasphemy.

6. The Tragedy That Stalks Your Very Life

1. David Augsberger, *Caring Enough to Not Forgive* (Scottsdale: Herald Press, 1981) pp. 9–10.

2. See my *Bonding: Relationships in the Image of God,* especially chapter 7, "Parents and Children: For Each Other."

3. Victor Davis, "Humperdinck endures part-time marriage," London Express Service, in *Hutchinson* (Kansas) *News,* Saturday, 8 June 1985, p. 17.

Appendix

Sexual Addiction: An Inventory from Sex Addicts Anonymous

_____ 1. Do you frequently feel compelled to have sex again and again within a short period of time?

_____ 2. Do you find it difficult to relate to other people because of thoughts or fantasies about being sexual with them?

_____ 3. Has your sexual behavior caused you either to seek help for it or made you feel scared or "different"—somehow alienated from people?

_____ 4. Have you ever tried to stop doing what you believed was wrong in your sexual behavior?

_____ 5. Do you sense that your sexual appetite is controlling you or that sexual images—either real or imagined—are controlling you?

_____ 6. Are you concerned about how much time you spend either in a sexual fantasy world or in setting up and acting out sexually?

_____ 7. Do you use sex to escape from worries or troubles or to "relax"? Do you use sex to hide other issues in your life?

_____ 8. Does your pursuit of sex interfere with your normal sexual relationship with your spouse or lover?

_____ 9. Have you ever tried to limit or control your sexual behavior? Have you made promises either to yourself or to your regular sexual partner and then broken those promises?

_____ 10. Do you find it almost impossible to have sex without resorting to certain kinds of sexual fantasies or memories of "unique" experiences?

_____ 11. Have you found yourself compelled by your sexual desires to the point where your regular sexual partner has rebelled?

_____ 12. Has your need for sex driven you to associate with persons or to spend time in places you would not normally choose?

_____ 13. Have you ever felt you'd be better off if you didn't need to give in to your sexual compulsions?

_____ 14. Do you frequently want to get away from a sex partner after having sex? Do you frequently feel remorse, shame, or guilt after a sexual encounter?

_____ 15. Has your job or school work suffered because of your sexual activities? Do you take time off from work to engage in sex?

_____ 16. Have you been arrested or nearly arrested because of your sexual activities? Have your sexual activities jeopardized your life goals?

_____ 17. Do your sexual activities include the risk of contracting disease or being maimed or killed by a violent sexual partner?

_____ 18. Has compulsive masturbation become a substitute for the kind of sexual relationship you want with your spouse or lover?

_____ 19. Has your effectiveness, productivity, concentration, or creativity decreased as your sexual activity has become more compulsive?

_____ 20. Has your sexual behavior ever made you feel hopeless or suicidal?

Prospectus

The inventory on the previous pages is published by S.A.A. as "Twenty Questions" as an "awareness test." There is no score or scoring. Any cluster of statements which strikes you as true of you might suggest that you consider seeking a healthier sexual pattern of thinking and living. The following paragraphs are excerpted, by permission, from basic S.A.A. documents:

Preamble

Sex Addicts Anonymous is a fellowship of women and men who share their experience, strength, and hope with each other that they may solve their common problem and help others recover from their sexual addictions. The only requirement for membership is a desire to stop compulsive sexual behavior. There are no dues or fees for S.A.A. membership; we are self-supporting through our own contributions. Sex Addicts Anonymous is not allied with any organization; does not wish to engage in any controversy; neither endorses nor opposes any causes. Sex Addicts Anonymous is not sex therapy or group therapy. Although there is no organizational affiliation between Alcoholics Anonymous and S.A.A., Sex Addicts Anonymous is based on the principles of A.A. Our primary purpose is to stay sexually healthy and help other sex addicts achieve freedom from compulsive sexual behavior.

How It Works

Rarely have we seen a person fail who has thoroughly followed our path. Those who do not recover are people who will not or cannot give themselves to this simple program. They cannot develop a manner of living which demands rigorous honesty. There are those, too, who suffer from grave emotional and mental disorders, but many of them do recover if they have the capacity to be honest.

Our stories disclose in a general way what we used to be like, what happened, and what we are like now. If you have decided you want what we have and are willing to go to any length to get it—then you are ready to take certain steps.

At some of these we balked. We thought we could find an easier, softer way. But we could not. With all the earnestness at our command, we beg of you to be fearless and thorough from the very start. Some of us have tried to hold on to our old ideas and the result was nil until we let go absolutely. Remember that we deal with sexual addiction—cunning, baffling, powerful! Without help it is too much for us. But there is One who has all power—that One is God. May you find God now!

Half measures availed us nothing. We stood at the turning point. We asked God's protection and care with complete abandon.

Here are the steps we took, which are suggested as a program of recovery. We—

1. Admitted we were powerless over our compulsive sexual behavior—that our lives had become unmanageable.
2. Came to believe that a Power greater than ourselves could restore us to sanity.
3. Made a decision to turn our will and our lives over to the care of God as we understood God.
4. Made a searching and fearless moral inventory of ourselves.
5. Admitted to God, to ourselves, and to another human being the exact nature of our wrongs.
6. Were entirely ready to have God remove all these defects of character.
7. Humbly asked God to remove our shortcomings.
8. Made a list of all persons we had harmed and became willing to make amends to them all.
9. Made direct amends to such people wherever possible, except when to do so would injure them or others.
10. Continued to take personal inventory and when we were wrong promptly admitted it.
11. Sought through prayer and meditation to improve our conscious contact with God as we understood God, praying only for knowledge of God's will for us and the power to carry that out.
12. Having had a spiritual awakening as the result of these steps, tried to carry this message to other sex addicts and to practice these principles in our lives.

Many of us exclaimed, "What an order! I can't go through with it!" Do not be discouraged. No one among us has been able to maintain anything like perfect adherence to these principles. We are not saints. The point is that we are willing to grow along spiritual lines. The principles we have set down are guides to progress. We claim spiritual progress rather than spiritual perfection.

Our understanding of sexual addiction and our personal adventures before and after make clear three pertinent ideas:

(a) We were sexually addicted and could not manage our own lives.
(b) Probably no human power could have relieved our addictive behavior.
(c) God could and would, if God were sought.

Sex Addicts Anonymous (S.A.A.)
P.O. Box 1532
Northbrook, Illinois 60062

Subject Index

Scripture Index

Genesis

2	63
3:16	63
3:8–10	27f.

Leviticus

20:10	130
2:7–8, 17–21	111

Deuteronomy

5:18	130
22	58, 106
23:14	n.67
24:1–4	64, 65, 67, 115

Judges

19:22–30	100f.

Ezra

10	65

Proverbs

6:26	48ff., 118

Song of Solomon

1:2; 1:5–10; 2:3–6; 6:4–9; 7:1–6	33ff.

Isaiah

54:1	5–6, 109
62:4–5	109

Jeremiah

31:3–4	21–22, 109

Ezekiel

16:32–34	99ff.

Matthew

5	67f.
5:27–28	128
5:29–30	133
5:32	66, 120
19	43, 61ff., 65, 66, 67, 77, 119

Mark

10:1–12	66
10:11–12	64

Luke

7:39–48	111
16:18	65

John

4:16–18	131
8:1–11	130
20	23, 139
21:15–17	15–16

1 Corinthians

5:4–5	104
6:5–6	122
6:9–11	69

Colossians

4:14	15

2 Timothy

2:22	129

DR. DONALD M. JOY is professor of Human Development and Christian Education at Asbury Theological Seminary in Wilmore, Kentucky. He received the M.A. degree in counseling from Southern Methodist University, and the Ph.D. from Indiana University. In addition, he teaches regularly in the Doctor of Education program at Talbot School of Theology in Los Angeles, and has been a guest professor at Princeton, Trinity Divinity School, and Wheaton graduate school. He has done a Word Educational Products videotape series on *Bonding:* Vol. I. The Mystery of Human Bonding; Pair Bonding: What God Joins Together. Vol. II. Creation, Adam, and Woman; On Splitting Adams! Vol. III. Sexual Integrity in a Pornographic Age; Grounds for Divorce? In addition to *Bonding,* he is the author of *Meaningful Learning in the Church* and *Moral Development Foundations.*